Changes
and
Choices

ALSO BY KATHY McCOY

Growing and Changing: A Handbook for Preteens
(with Charles Wibbelsman, M.D.)

The New Teenage Body Book
(with Charles Wibbelsman, M.D.)

Solo Parenting: Your Essential Guide

Coping With Teenage Depression

The Teenage Body Book Guide to Sexuality

The Teenage Body Book Guide to Dating

The Teenage Survival Guide

Changes and Choices: A JUNIOR HIGH SURVIVAL GUIDE

Kathy McCoy

A PERIGEE BOOK

Perigee Books
are published by
The Putnam Publishing Group
200 Madison Avenue
New York, NY 10016

Library of Congress Cataloging-in-Publication Data

McCoy, Kathy, date.
    Changes and choices: a junior high survival guide / by Kathy
McCoy.
        p.   cm.
    Summary: A guide to surviving socially and psychologically such
concerns as crushes, first love, embarrassment, changing families,
making choices, and peer competition.
    1. Junior high school students—United States—Attitudes—Juvenile
literature.   2. Adolescence—United States—Juvenile literature.
    [1. Conduct of life.   2. Adolescence.]   I. Title.
LB1135.M37   1989   89-8414   CIP   AC
373.2'36—dc20
ISBN 0-399-51566-6

Printed in the United States of America

1   2   3   4   5   6   7   8   9   10

SPECIAL THANKS TO:

Gene Brissie

Alice Fried Martell

Lillian Spina

Contents

Introduction:
Your Changing World

I'm going to be starting junior high this year and I don't know what to expect. It's kind of exciting, but it might be hard, too, going from being the class everyone looks up to at school to being the little kids again. How can I act so that people won't treat me like a little kid?

Jason R.

My dad says that junior high is fun and will be the start of my being more like an adult. My mom says that junior high is the one argument she has against reincarnation: If she has to go through junior high again, she'd rather not have another life. My older friends talk about it in really different ways, too: Some are totally happy and others hate it. What can I do to make it a good experience for me? How can I get off to a good start so I don't hate it—or the other people don't hate me?

Heather H.

Junior high. These words can bring excitement—or strike terror—into the hearts of those who look forward to starting this special time of life, those who are now in junior high, and those who look back and remember.

Like so many other life experiences, junior high can have its positive *and* negative sides. But these years are unique for a couple of reasons.

First, if you are moving from sixth grade at an elementary school to seventh grade at a junior high, this may well be one of the most stressful—and exciting—academic changes you'll experience. Why? Because going to junior high involves so many different changes in your life. You are going from the more personal atmosphere of elementary school with one teacher and one classroom to a larger, more impersonal and demanding school setting where you not only have to remember your locker combination right from the start, but also will be changing teachers and classrooms every period. You have been looked up to by younger kids in grade school, but now you're going to be the youngest class at your new school. You're making the leap from childhood to young adulthood in so many ways. You're facing new academic expectations. Grades and achievements take on new importance to the adults in your life (if not to you) as they remind you of the importance of getting

9

well prepared for high school and thinking ahead to college and/or your future career. You may also be experiencing new pressures to be popular and to be liked by the opposite sex. Friends are more important than ever before, and having someone special to love who, preferably, loves you back is suddenly a vital, if sometimes elusive, part of your changing world.

Second, your feelings are changing. Quite often, these feelings seem to be at war with one another. For example, sometimes you may feel totally independent and resent your parents' rules and advice. Yet at other times, you feel a sudden need to be a little kid again, to have your parents' protection for a while longer. (This is not only confusing for you, but also for your parents!) You may be suddenly very critical of your parents and other people in your family, even though you really love them. It may be harder to express love to your family and embarrassing when they show love to you, like hugging you in front of your friends, even though you really need their love. You may be more critical of yourself these days, too: worrying about saying or doing something dumb and being made fun of by everyone, wanting to be attractive and feeling you fall short for any number of reasons, and wondering if you can ever be the kind of person you really want to be. You may feel shy in new situations, especially with the opposite sex. You may have times of loneliness. Maybe it's because you don't have a boyfriend or girlfriend or a special best friend. Maybe it's because you feel different from your classmates. Maybe it's hard to know the reason. But you know that you feel very alone sometimes. And at the same time you feel a greater need for privacy than ever before. You don't like to have your parents or anyone (except maybe a best friend) know everything about you.

Third, your body is changing and that, in itself, can be both exciting and scary and sometimes embarrassing. This is a time when you want to feel normal, when you want to fit in with your friends. Yet, at no time in your life to come will you and your friends look so different from each other than you do right now. Some people in junior high still look like little kids, even though inside they may *feel* quite mature. Others may look almost grown, maybe years older than they *feel* inside. Each person has his or her own normal timetable for growth. (Often, this timetable matches that of one of your parents'. If you're an early bloomer, a late bloomer, or somewhere in between, it could simply be part of your genetic inheritance.) So whether you start developing earlier than most of your friends, or later, or right along with the majority, you're still normal. Inheriting your growth timetable is like getting your father's nose or your mother's blue eyes. Some people start to grow and mature into adolescents as early as fourth or fifth grade. Others may be in high school before they start to look like teenagers. And even though this is normal for them, it can be hard to look different from a lot of your friends.

You'll experience one of the toughest differences in growth timetables in junior high. That's when your individual differences are most obvious. And two common junior high facts of life make these differences even more obvious. First, you will be showering and changing for gym class with your classmates, where all the differences in development are there for everyone to see and compare. Second, it's quite common for boys, on the average, to lag a little behind girls in physical development. So it's not at all unusual to see girls taller and more mature looking (and sometimes acting more mature as well) at junior high dances. While this can all cause some temporary discomfort, you *can* survive it all with good feelings about yourself and others, too.

That is what this book is all about: helping you to cope with the unique problems of being in your early teens *and* helping you to discover all the unique joys of being who you are and the age you happen to be.

There *are* a lot of joys you'll find in these junior high years: the beginning of independence, falling in love, perhaps for the first time, special friendships, finding out more all the time about the special person you're growing to be, and finding your own dreams and goals for the future. All of these experiences—and more—can make your changing world an exciting place to be!

CHAPTER ONE

Your Changing Feelings

Sometimes I don't know what to do about my feelings. I just turned 13 and wonder if it's normal to feel really up part of the day and then, if something happens or maybe for no reason at all, to feel like everything in my life is horrible. I also get mad at my mom a lot and say things I don't really mean, except at the time. I told her I hated her when I was upset yesterday, but I really love her. How do I show her I'm sorry and that I love her without getting into an argument or something?

Jessica P.

What can you do if you feel you don't fit in anywhere? I think sometimes that I worry and have more problems than a lot of people. I don't fit in with the smart kids or the rad group or the geeks. I get jealous of kids who are popular, have great personalities, and look fantastic. I'm scared of people making fun of me. I get my feelings hurt easily. I feel lonely a lot. But I can't talk to anyone about these feelings. What can I do to feel better?

L.J.

There are a lot of new and confusing feelings you may have right now.

Sometimes these feel good—like being proud of learning something new or accomplishing something you could never do before or falling in love.

But some of the feelings are painful ones and may be taking on new importance now that you're older. Some of these feelings may come from the expectations others, like parents or teachers or your classmates, may have of you. Some come from your own feelings of confusion or discomfort about your changing body, your family, your friends or lack of friends, your growing personality, and your opinion of yourself.

Unfortunately, the feelings that hurt are quite often the ones that are hard to talk about. Sometimes you can't quite describe the feeling so another person can understand. You may be ashamed of how you feel or think that this feeling is so strange or unusual that no one could possibly understand. And so you keep your thoughts to yourself. But keeping quiet about or trying to ignore your feelings doesn't make them go away.

It helps to talk. It helps to think about your painful feelings to see why they're happening and how you can begin to change the way you feel or see yourself. It helps to take action.

It may also help to know that, whatever you're feeling, you're not alone!

The following are some of the most common troubling feelings expressed by people in their early teens. Maybe you'll recognize some of your own feelings—and discover some ideas for feeling better about yourself and your changing world— among them.

FEELING INFERIOR AND SELF-CRITICAL

Everyone hates me. I just know it. I'm not cute or smart or especially fun to be with. I try to be nice, but I always seem to say the wrong thing or something. Everyone has a best friend but me. Everyone is doing better than me in every way. Will it always be this way? I hate it! What can I do?

"Sad Seventh Grader"

Feeling inferior is one of the most painful feelings you can have.

Like "Sad," you may be feeling that you aren't as good as anyone you know in any way. Or you may feel good about yourself in some areas of your life, but not in others.

For example, you may think, "Well, I'm fairly smart and I know I'm a good friend. But I hate the way I look." And you get so upset about what you think are your physical shortcomings that it's hard to remember what's so good about being you.

Or maybe you feel inferior because people expect so much of you. You may get down on yourself because you feel you can't possibly measure up to the expectations your parents or your friends have for you.

Maybe you feel bad about yourself because you feel you make more mistakes than most people you know, or because you feel shy and awkward around boys (or girls).

Maybe you feel that if you can't be perfect, if you can't be Number One in everything, if you can't be the most attractive, the smartest, the most popular person, you're totally worthless. This "all or nothing" thinking can trap a lot of really terrific people—maybe you among them—into feeling inferior instead of enjoying their wonderful, if imperfect, uniqueness.

Feeling inferior can come as the result of other people teasing, criticizing, or seeming to ignore you. But the good news is that, whether your feelings of inferiority come entirely from your own thoughts about yourself or from the way others act toward you, *you* can change all this!

You need to realize that, even if your painful feelings come because of the actions of others, *you* are still involved in the process—so you can change it!

Eleanor Roosevelt once said, "No one can make you feel inferior without your consent."

And it's true! That explains why some people can hear rude comments from someone and just say, "Get lost!" without taking in the hurtful message of the words, and why others automatically accept taunts and criticisms from others as the absolute truth about themselves.

Which sounds like you?

If you're still not sure, try taking the following test.

Answering "Yes" to any of the following questions can be a clue that you are allowing other people to attack you or that you are using them to reinforce your own bad feelings about yourself. The more "Yes" answers you have, the more serious this problem is for you.

1. Do you immediately assume, when you walk past a group of schoolmates and they start whispering or laughing, that they're laughing at you?
2. If you hear that a classmate doesn't like you, does it ruin your day and make you feel worthless and totally unloved? Do you really need to have *everyone* like you?
3. If someone criticizes you, do you automatically assume he or she is right?
4. Do you fantasize a lot about being someone else and feel mostly unhappy about being you?
5. Do you hang around with people who say mean things to you, play tricks on you, stand you up and otherwise treat you like a nonperson?
6. Do you stay with such "friends" because you feel so bad about yourself that you think even friends like these are better than no friends at all?
7. Do you feel like a complete failure if you aren't first in everything? Do you see coming in second or being a runner-up as a total disaster? Do you think you're nothing if . . . you don't have a boyfriend (or girlfriend) . . . if you make a lower grade than you expected (or your parents expected) . . . or if you don't make a team?
8. Do you pick on yourself for every little mistake or imperfection, going on and on to yourself about how stupid or clumsy or unattractive you are?
9. Do you do things that hurt you—like smoking or drinking too much or eating too much or too little—because you need to be accepted by others who do the same, or because this is the only way you know to deal with the pain and loneliness you feel?
10. Do you say "If only" a lot? As in: "If only I had someone of my very own to love . . . If only I could be beautiful (or handsome) . . . If only my parents were rich . . . If only I had a car . . ." What your *If only*'s are saying is that you're nothing without these elusive goals, that you can't feel happy or successful or worthwhile unless you have these things.

The truth is, though, that you *can* feel good about yourself even if you aren't unusually attractive or rich or popular or brilliant. Those are just extras some happy (and unhappy) people have. You can feel good about yourself even if others laugh or make fun of you sometimes.

How can you do this? Try some (or all) of the following to get off to a good start!

Stop Trying to Please Everyone Else and Start Pleasing Yourself. This doesn't mean being selfish or thoughtless. It means asking yourself, "What do *I* really want? What do I enjoy most? What makes me feel good about myself?"

For example, Bob, an eighth grader, enjoys playing his guitar and singing, but his parents and sister make fun of him and tell him he has a horrible singing voice.

Bob has been feeling really low for two reasons: being made fun of by his family and feeling he has to give up a hobby that gives him a lot of pleasure.

He might feel better if he concentrated on the pleasure his music gives him. Whether or not he has a wonderful voice (and most people don't), he can still do what he likes. Maybe he needs to sing when other family members aren't home. Maybe he needs to close the door of his room when he's playing and singing. Maybe he could talk to his family and say something like, "I realize that you think I don't have a good singing voice, but I really enjoy playing the guitar and singing. How can I do what I enjoy so much without bothering any of you?"

Your feelings and pleasures and interests are important. As long as you can pursue them without hurting yourself or others, doing so will help you to feel better about yourself.

You can also please yourself by being helpful and nice to others in your own way. This is a lot different from running around trying to please everyone and not taking care of your own feelings. This way, you choose to be nice or helpful because that's the way you are, because it reinforces your own good feelings about yourself. So, even if other people don't react with friendship or gratitude, you still feel good about yourself because you behaved the way you wanted to behave. When you concentrate on meeting your own expectations and being true to your own feelings, you will find it easier to say "No" to people who try to take unfair advantage of you or to force you to do things you don't want to do. And being able to say "No" will also help you to feel better about saying "Yes" to other people or situations.

Instead of turning people off, your honesty and sincerity may win you more friends. But, most important, you will begin to build your own self-respect.

Be As Gentle With Yourself As You Are With Your Best Friend (*or the Person You Would Like to Have As a Best Friend*). Think about how you criticize yourself. Would you *dare* talk that way, would you even *think* of talking that way to a dear friend?

What would you do if your friend told you she felt bad about herself? Wouldn't you point out all her good qualities? Wouldn't you be surprised at how critical she is of things about herself that aren't even evident to or a problem for others? Why can't you be just as loving and gentle with yourself? What's true for your friend is also true for you: You have many more good qualities than faults. And you're probably your own worst critic.

The early teens are a time of major self-criticism. Why? Because your body changes are heightening your awareness of your physical assets and shortcomings. And, as you grow in awareness, you are also more tuned in to your own and other people's limitations.

For example, until fairly recently, you might have thought that your parents knew everything. Now you may get the feeling that sometimes (maybe a lot of times) they're incredibly out of it.

And, until recently, you may not have been quite so aware of what you now consider to be major faults of your own: an accent, a funny laugh, a tendency to be clumsy, hair that's curly or straight or just dull, a body that's not fashionably thin or that is *too* thin. You may have always had these qualities, but now they're bothering you because you've become self-conscious. You're more aware of your limitations.

This awareness can help you to make positive changes. It can help you to discover your uniqueness and to accept these qualities simply as part of the loveable person you are. It can also hurt if you become too focused on what you see as the negative, so supercritical of yourself that you lose sight of everything that's good and wonderful and loveable about you.

So be a dear friend to yourself. Stop beating up on yourself for not being a superstar at sports or music or socializing, and let yourself enjoy these and other pursuits in your own way.

For example, Jan has taken clarinet lessons all through school and is competent, but not outstanding. For a while, in seventh grade, she really felt bad when she realized how much more talent some of the others in the school band happened to have. But she decided to stick with it because she loved being part of the band and, this year, she has become an especially valuable member. No, not because of her music. She's still far from the best musician. But Jan has a wonderful knack for organization and fundraising. She has been the fundraising champ this year and has been a big help in raising money for the band to travel to several competitions and a major parade appearance.

"I could have sat around tearing myself down because I'm not considered one of the big talents musically," she says. "But I decided to do what I would do for a friend in this spot. I asked myself what I'm *really* good at and used that talent to help the band. Instead of just concentrating on what I don't have, I started thinking about ways I'm special and can be an important part of the band. So now I get to play the clarinet *and* do what I do best."

Her classmate Tom is in a similar position. He loves sports, but isn't a varsity-level player. But, as a timekeeper and assistant trainer for several varsity teams at his school, Tom is an important part of his school's athletic program. As gently as a friend would, he began by saying to himself, "Well, you didn't make the team as a player. That's too bad. I know you're disappointed. But, hey, you love sports and love being a part of a team. Why not bring your sports knowledge and enthusiasm to the team in another way?"

If Tom hadn't been hired as a trainer and timekeeper, he might have been an enthusiastic fan, cheering the team to victory (instead of hating himself for not being a part of it). You can turn what looks like failure into a triumph if you're a friend to yourself. Instead of criticism, give yourself encouragement. Instead of labeling yourself a failure, look for the unique talents you can develop and enjoy.

Maybe you're convinced that you have no special talents. You might say, "I'm not talented or terrific in any of the ways that count." Wait a minute! Would you say something like that to a friend?? Wouldn't you reassure your friend by telling him or her everything that is *right* about him or her?

Be a friend to yourself. You have so many good qualities. Even the ones that you think are unimportant really *do* count!

For example, maybe you're patient and kind. Maybe you are good about keeping promises and secrets. Maybe you're the sort of person others turn to when they're sad or afraid *or* have good news to share. Maybe you're a fantastic baby-sitter or a curious person with an active intelligence and interest in many different topics. Maybe you're the best person you know at keeping other people's secrets. Respecting other people's privacy and feelings is a *very* important part of being a good friend. Maybe you see life from a creative perspective and feel things deeply. This can mean that you're sensitive to your own and others' feelings.

Don't Automatically Assume That Others Are Right Just Because They Say So. Criticisms can be unfair. Opinions are just a reflection of someone else's feelings, not an absolute fact. Others' expectations for you can be unrealistic.

So just because someone tells you something about yourself that makes you feel inferior or disliked, don't accept this without question. Ask *yourself* if this makes any sense at all. If you could step outside yourself and be your best friend, would you agree with the comments at all? A little bit? Is this something about yourself that you can change? Do you even *want* to change something just because someone else thinks you should?

An important part of growing toward confident independence is developing your own point of view and knowing, deep down, what's really right for you. Your opinions count a lot. You have a right to question others' expectations of you as well as your own. You don't have to take to heart any criticisms that just don't make sense to you. Don't assume you're always wrong and someone else is always right—especially when it comes to negative opinions about *you*!

Keep in mind that constructive criticism has a strong element of loving concern. The other person loves and accepts you as you are—and just wants to help you to be even better or learn something new or avoid a painful mistake.

Nonconstructive criticism just tears you down and is quite often an attempt to undermine whatever self-confidence or sense of accomplishment you might have.

And *that's* wrong—even if there is a little bit of truth to the hurtful words.

Give Yourself a Break!! Do you expect perfection: Does an "A-minus" equal total failure, does one rude remark cancel out every good thing that happened to you last week? If you're not the most popular, most talented, most intelligent, most attractive person at school, does that mean you're a nobody? If this all sounds familiar, you may be doing a very good job of making yourself feel miserable and inferior—all by yourself!

Ease up. And think about it. No one can be perfect. No one can win all the time. No one can be loved and admired by everyone. It's true that some people have more friends than others. But quantity isn't everything. The quality of the friendships matter most. And no one—*no one*—can be loved by everyone.

If you're like most people, you will have some friends (and family members) who really love you, people you can talk with about anything. Then you will have some fun, but less intimate, friends, who think you're a nice person, but who don't know you as well. And there will be some other people at school who hardly know you but still think you're an okay person. A few others might not like you at all for reasons all their own, some of which may have nothing directly to do with you. And a lot of people at school will be pretty indifferent to you. This indifference, which you may see as dislike for you, has little to do with you personally. Most people are so concerned about themselves that they have a fairly limited amount of emotional energy left over to become deeply involved with too many other people. When you stop to think about it, you may feel the same way, too.

Expecting perfection in other ways is equally unrealistic. Some people *do* make straight "A's," but that doesn't mean they don't make mistakes. Mistakes can be valuable learning opportunities. There are very few things you can do just right the first time around. Even Olympic athletes mess up, have bad days, and disappointments. So when you have days like that or make a mistake, give yourself a break. Instead of putting yourself down for being imperfect, ask yourself, "What can I learn from this?" Give yourself credit for trying. And think about what you can *realistically* expect from yourself or from a certain situation. You're going to make mistakes. You're going to be very good at some skills and not so good at others. And with some things, you simply need more time to grow as a person. Being mature in some ways and immature in other ways is a natural way for you to be right now. Some of what bothers you about yourself—like getting flustered and not knowing what to say around someone of the opposite sex—is, most likely, a temporary way of being. As you become more comfortable with yourself as a new young adult, you'll find that you'll be more at ease with others as well.

Be gentle with yourself. You can be a terrible tennis player and still be loved. You can stammer over a speech at a school assembly—even forget the whole speech and just stand there with your face getting redder by the second—and somehow survive and even laugh about it later. No one is going to hate you because you were nervous or scared or unprepared. You can handle a situation badly, say something thoughtless to a friend and learn from it—and a sincere apology, an offer to make it up to him or her and the wisdom not to repeat such mistakes—can even deepen a friendship.

Lovingly Accept Yourself—Faults and All—As You Are Right Now. That is the only way you can grow to become the best you can be. That is the only way others will come to accept and like you. When you can love the fool in yourself as well as the wise person, you will be able to learn from mistakes, to laugh at yourself, to pick yourself up from disappointments and go on. And other people are drawn to people like that: who know their limitations, have a good sense of humor, and who don't let setbacks ruin anything—from a day to a friendship.

ANGER

People at school make me mad. And I always do something really embarrassing like cry or make a big scene. How can I improve my temper, even when someone else is being awful, so people don't think I'm the awful one?

Jessica D.

Why do I do this: have a bad day at school and then come home and yell at my brother or be sort of rude (like ignoring) my mom? I can't stop being angry sometimes. And it hurts people who have nothing to do with me being angry. What can I do about this?

Scott Y.

When I get upset with someone over something, I can't tell them! I just hurt a bunch inside and don't say anything, but I stay upset for a long time. It makes me feel awful! How can I change?

Kate A.

Do you:

- Get angry with people you love as well as with those you don't like?
- Feel angry when your mom unfairly accuses you of eating a piece of the apple pie she made for the bake sale (without checking out the crumbs on your little sister's face)?
- Get mad when someone at school says something rude or spreads lies about you?
- Feel angry at someone—from a parent to a pet—who has died, even though you miss this person a lot and know he or she loved you and wouldn't have left you, given a choice?
- Get furious and hurt when your (former) best friend says she has a new best friend and doesn't want to hang around with you anymore?
- Find yourself angry and disappointed when your dad, who promised he'd stop smoking on New Year's Day, starts up again only four days later?

Well, guess what? You're normal!

Anger is simply a natural, human emotion. It isn't bad. It doesn't signal a lack of love or caring. Quite the opposite. You may find you get maddest at those closest to you.

So you may find yourself getting furious with those you love for treating you unfairly, for hurting themselves with a bad habit, for not being there when you need them. It's quite common, when someone close to you dies, to feel a lot of anger in with your grief, as you rage at that person for leaving you, even though you know it couldn't be helped.

And you can get pretty angry with people you *don't* love, too, if they are nasty or inconsiderate or somehow stand in the way of something you want to achieve (like the English teacher who seems to be allergic to any essay that has a trace of creativity or originality of thought, or that creep who takes pleasure in running around trying to "steal" everyone else's boyfriends).

Being angry is a natural reaction in these situations, too.

So anger itself isn't a problem. It can alert you to danger or to a need for change. It can be a source of energy, helping you to make changes in your life or to get through a really tough time.

The problem may well be, then, how you *express* or *don't* express your anger.

Maybe you lose control and attack *everyone* (even innocent bystanders) when you're angry.

Maybe you can't express your feelings to the person who upsets you, but you lash out at other people you feel are safe targets: people who are younger or weaker or who love you so much (or are at least related to you) so that it would be hard for them to lash back or to reject you forever.

Maybe you just hold your anger in—hurting a lot, feeling bad about yourself because you can't stand up to someone. Maybe, too, these held-in feelings are causing you to get stomachaches or headaches or feel depressed. Maybe they cause you to do hurtful things to yourself like drink or take drugs or overeat just to calm down.

Remember: You can't keep yourself from getting angry, but you *do* have a choice about how you will express and/or cope with your anger. And that can make a big difference!

How can you change your angry behavior?

Express Your Anger Clearly But Calmly at the Time to the Person Involved—Whenever Possible. This is the choice that will help you to grow and to keep others from pinpointing you as a possible victim.

If you have a tendency to cry or to get so enraged that you're totally irrational, take some deep breaths or count to 10 (or 20!) and then speak up. Or you may need to wait awhile and approach the person again, when you feel calmer and more able to discuss your feelings.

It's best not to attack the other person and heap insult upon insult. You're more likely to resolve this problem if you tell the other person that you're angry and why. Talk about your *feelings* instead of making accusations.

For example, if you have a friend who is great when you're alone together, but who acts mean to you when someone else is around (mostly to show off or to make sure she is liked best), you might say, "I feel angry when you act like my best friend in private and then say things that hurt my feelings in front of other people." This tells her what you're feeling and why—and gives her a clue about changing her behavior if she's willing.

This can be much better for everyone concerned than just losing it and yelling, "You're a total jerk! I hate you! I'm never going to speak to you again!" That closes off communication pretty effectively, and, especially if it comes from long, accumulated hurt and anger instead of as a reaction to this one situation, may leave everyone thinking, "Wow! What's the matter with *her*? Why is she so upset over something so minor?"

If You Find Yourself Lashing Out at Someone Else, Stop, Apologize, and Report Your Feelings. This can help break a hurtful pattern of misdirecting your anger to someone totally innocent.

For example, Mike was having a hard time making friends at his new school when he was in seventh grade. Because he was younger and shorter than a lot of his classmates, he got teased a lot. Most days that fall, he came home from school in an angry mood. He'd sulk and throw things and snap at his sister until his mom came home from work. Then, when she asked how his day had been, he'd yell at her and stomp off to his room for more sulking. This was making his whole life—at school *and* at home—pretty grim.

So he decided to try a new approach. First, he vowed to stop taking his anger out on his family. So when his mom would ask about the day, he'd say, "I'm feeling angry because I had another hard day. I got teased and someone started a fight with me at gym and we both got punished. I'm upset and feel like just going to my room for a while. Maybe we could talk about this later, Mom, after I calm down." His mother agreed and, when they talked later, she helped him to find ways to cope with what was happening at school. Things improved at home first and, gradually, at school. But Mike's new beginning started when he got control of his anger and began to talk about it.

If You Can't Tell Anyone How You Feel Right Now, Do Something Good for Yourself That Will Help Calm You Down and Get Rid of the Anger. Drinking, drug use, overeating, or other unhealthy habits don't count. What you need to do is something that will help to get rid of some of the angry energy and clear your mind.

What can help? You might think about:

- Doing some vigorous exercise. If you're really angry, try something that involves hitting—like tennis or racquetball or squash. Or run until you're exhausted. The point is to get rid of all that angry energy and tension.
- Taking a long walk, preferably in an area that you enjoy. Breathe deeply and expel some angry feelings each time you exhale. Look around and notice something beautiful or funny or interesting.
- Trying to accomplish something you've been putting off, like cleaning your room or mowing the lawn. The physical exertion can help and so can the sense of relief and accomplishment when you find you've done something you've been dreading—at a time when you didn't feel great anyway. It really can help you to feel better.
- Writing a letter to the other person and saying exactly how you feel. Then tear it up.
- Writing your feelings down in a journal or diary. It can really help you to know what you're feeling—and to get some of these angry feelings out of your system.
- Unleashing your emotions in private: Scream into your pillow, beat on your pillow, cry. Have a private tantrum. That might clear your head so that you can calm down and do something constructive about your situation.

JEALOUSY

I feel bad a lot of the time because I'm so jealous. I'm jealous of the people in the in-group at school because they're popular and have nice clothes and are dating already. I don't even have a boyfriend. I'm jealous of my little sister, who's three years old, because everyone in the family goes on about how cute she is and how perfect she is, and they just criticize me or say I'm at that awkward age. (I just turned 13.) I'm even jealous of my best friend because she does so well in school without having to study as much as I do. How can I start feeling better?

                                                                    Jamie T.

Jealousy is a very common feeling and can strike at any age and in a variety of circumstances.

Sometimes, especially at times in your life when you feel things aren't going well for you, you can feel jealous a lot of the time, like Jamie does. Maybe it seems like everyone has wonderful things or special qualities that you don't have. And you feel angry, upset, and deprived. And, if you're like a lot of people, you're feeling guilty for being jealous, especially if you're jealous of someone you love.

For example, John is upset with himself for being jealous of his buddy Brian for making the football team when he didn't. "I should be happy for him and I guess I am, in a way," he says. "But I'm more unhappy that I didn't make it. Does this mean I'm not a good friend?"

No. It just means that John has very human feelings and is experiencing disappointment of his own. It may take time for him to get over this and to feel truly happy for his friend.

Emily, an eighth grader who has liked her classmate Ted since fifth grade and has been going out with him for several months, finds herself feeling jealous in a different way: She feels upset when Ted even *looks* at another girl or says, "Hi." If she sees him talking to someone else, she feels panicky inside, wondering whether this means he likes someone else more. Ironically, Emily's fear of losing Ted may be pushing him away. Lately, he has complained about her jealousy and possessiveness and has suggested that they keep dating, but start seeing other people. Emily listens with tears in her eyes, thinking that her worst fears are about to come true.

What can *you* do to tame jealousy before it makes your worst fears a reality? How can you keep this troubling feeling from interfering with important relationships and your own happiness?

Here are a few suggestions:

Accept Your Jealousy and Learn Something From It. Once you stop putting yourself down for feeling jealous, you can ask yourself, "What is this feeling telling me? What can I learn from it?"

Your jealousy may give you a clue about changes you want to make in your own life.

It could be that, if you feel everyone has a better life than you do, your self-esteem isn't what it could be. You may be overlooking your special qualities and your unique blessings. You may need to start looking at what you have (that *other* people may envy), instead of what you don't have.

Mandy, for example, has been secretly jealous of her friend Chris since they met last year in seventh grade. "Chris is a nice person and all," she says, "but it's hard for me to deal with the fact that her parents are so rich and she has all these great clothes and has been to Europe a bunch of times. They live in this huge house and Chris is going to get a car for her sixteenth birthday in three years. I get embarrassed when my mom picks me up in her horrible looking ten-year-old-station wagon and offers Chris a ride, too."

But recently Chris surprised Mandy by expressing a little envy of her own. "I really like your mom," she said. "She's so nice and down to earth and makes me feel so comfortable. She always has time to do things with you. My mom is busy all the time. And neither of my parents are *comfortable* kinds of people, you know, that you can just talk to like a person can with your mom. You're really lucky!"

So when you feel jealousy, this may be a sign that you're overlooking what's right in your own life.

Or maybe it's a sign that there is something you need to change.

If you're jealous because someone else always looks great, you can improve your own look. Study magazines for beauty tips and fashion advice. (You don't have to spend lots of money to get a new look. It may just involve wearing the clothes you already have with a new accessory or two or figuring out some great-looking combinations.)

If you envy someone else's lean, healthy looks, you can have your own version of that look, too, if you're willing to work at it. While body shapes are different (some people are naturally thinner and more angular in shape than others), you can look your best if you eat balanced, nutritious meals, go easy on the junk food, and get plenty of exercise. Those of us who have naturally more rounded shapes may have to work at fitness and weight control more than someone who was born to be willowy, but we all have our own best look—and by living a healthy lifestyle, you can find yours.

If you're jealous of someone's good grades and ashamed of your own, you can do something about this, too. While some people will always make top grades, seemingly without effort, and some people will have to study harder to do well, doing your best, whatever that may be, will help you to feel better. Maybe this means studying more or organizing your time better or asking for help when you need it.

If you're upset because someone has more friends than you do, ask yourself how *you* can be a better friend to others. By concentrating on improving your own friendship skills, you can learn and grow from your initial jealous feelings. Maybe, too, you need to look beyond your immediate class or school for friends who will share some of your special interests or values. There may be friendship possibilities in your church group or through volunteer work or in special interest groups or activities outside of school.

The point is: Jealous feelings can give you valuable clues about what you might want to change in your life—and what's right about your life that you just haven't noticed.

Ask Yourself What Others Might Envy in You—and Discover (Or Rediscover) the Positive Qualities in Your Life. Sometimes you may feel that you're the only person who experiences jealousy and who lacks the essentials for happiness. But the fact is, we *all* have what we need to be happy, if we can just see and accept this.

You can't know what it's like to live another person's life—and if you could, chances are you might not be so ready to trade everything with another. Most people, even those whose lives seem perfect, have their problems, their disappointments, and their insecurities. You know someone who doesn't? Don't be too sure.

I remember feeling that way about Doreen, a girl I knew in ninth grade. Doreen seemed to have it all—or, at least, everything I didn't have. She was really cute and outgoing. Her hair and makeup and clothes were always *perfect*. She was a cheerleader and a certified member of the in-group. She had a terrific boyfriend. And to top it all off (if you can stand any more!), because she lived some distance from the school and had no other means of transportation, she had a special *driver's license* permitting her to drive to and from school and her *own* car! The surest sign of being "in" at my school was to hang out around Doreen's car at lunchtime and to eat lunch *in* her car was the ultimate.

I ran into Doreen a few years ago and we impulsively decided to have lunch together and talk (something we had never done in school). No, Doreen's life hadn't turned awful and boring and downright miserable after her junior high triumphs. She was happily married to her terrific boyfriend, had a little daughter, and a career she enjoyed. She was still pretty and cheerful and outgoing. But she said something that surprised me. "I used to envy you in school," she said.

I stared at her. It had to be a joke. I waited for the punch line. And I remembered my shyness, my lack of confidence, my curly hair that refused to go into the smooth, sleek style so popular in our junior high years, my anguish over the guys who thought I was a great pal but who usually asked someone else to a special dance. "You're kidding," I said with a suspicious little smile.

"No!" Doreen looked absolutely serious. "People respected you because you were smart. You seemed very sure of yourself in a quiet way. I think people always thought of me as silly and stupid. Nobody took me seriously. And I always thought a lot of people liked me just because of the car or because I had a boyfriend who had a lot of good male friends who might be potential dates for them. Lots of times, I felt no one liked me for *me* and that no one thought I had any substance. And that hurt."

So you never know . . .

It's true that you can't see yourself as others see you—and how others see you may or may not be totally accurate anyway. But it can help to look at what you *do* have. You're very special in your own way. What does your best friend like most about you? If you don't know, take the risk of asking him or her. What do you like most about yourself? What brings you pleasure? What skills or qualities do you have that help you to feel good about yourself? These don't have to be the obvious, like being on a team or winning a prize or good grades or anything like that. Maybe you're a good, compassionate friend. Maybe you really know how to listen. Maybe you have a terrific sense of humor. Maybe you have a good, generous spirit and find joy in helping others at home, at school, or through volunteer work. Maybe you feel things deeply and are growing to understand your own feelings—and those of others—in new ways.

If you really think about it, you have a lot of blessings—and the potential for much more happiness and growth—in your life right now!

Don't Let Jealousy Come Between You and Those You Love. Jealousy can destroy relationships. It can mean squeezing the life out of a love relationship because you're so afraid of losing a boyfriend or a girlfriend to another. It can mean letting envious feelings poison the good feelings you have for a friend or a sibling.

If this sounds painfully familiar to you, the first thing you need to do is to reassure yourself that you have a lot to offer and the love of another can't be lost so easily, but if, somehow, it is, you will survive. Knowing that you can live *without* someone special to you can, in fact, make the relationship more likely to endure simply because you will trust him or her enough to have time, friends, and a life of his or her own. Holding on too tight in a relationship—whether a romantic one or a friendship—is like squeezing a handful of sand. The tighter you squeeze, the faster it runs through your fingers. But if you cup it gently, giving it a special space all its own, it stays.

If, like Jamie, you're feeling jealous of an attention-getting sibling (whether this sibling is younger and cuter, older, and more accomplished or ill, injured, or handicapped and getting the lion's share of parental time), it's important to remember that, quite often, this is temporary or cyclical and may have little, if anything, to do with your value as a person. A lot of people do find three-year-olds irresistible, but don't know quite how to relate to 13-year-olds. You may well catch up to an older sibling in time or develop special talents and skills of your own. And a sibling who gets more parental attention because of an illness or a special problem is not necessarily loved more. Many parents claim to love their children equally, but in different ways, and claim that a greater helping of love is available to the child who needs it most at the moment. If you don't feel your parents' love or if you feel unfairly compared to a sibling, say something to them about this in a respectful way. Just tell them your feelings.

You might say, for example: "I feel hurt and upset when you compare me with Amy. I'm a different person. And I need you to see how I'm special in my own way and help me to become better in my own way, too."

If your parents genuinely seem to prefer a sibling and really aren't available to you, there *is* an alternative to feeling shut out and jealous. You can find other adults to give you the attention and guidance that your parents seem unwilling or unable to give you. Perhaps these people might include other relatives, a family friend, a neighbor, a favorite teacher. There are people who will be there for you and will help you, if you look around and reach out to them.

SHYNESS

I'm unbelievably shy and it has made me real unpopular in sixth grade. I don't want the same thing to happen when I start junior high in two months. How can I stop being shy? Just the thought of talking to new people gets me scared!!

Andrea B.

If you're shy with adults, like teachers, but not with your friends, does that make you shy—or not? I have a hard time meeting people, but once I know them I'm not shy at all. Am I still a shy person?

Kevin H.

If, like Kevin and Andrea, you feel shy at times, you're not at all unusual—even if you *feel* painfully different at times!

Shyness is common at this age—when you're facing so many changes: physically, socially, and in your school setting. And feeling shy can be especially painful at this time when you want so much to be liked and accepted by your classmates.

People can be shy in different ways. Some people, like Andrea, feel shy most of the time while others, like Kevin, just feel shy with people at first or with certain kinds of people—like teachers or other authority figures or adults in general. Maybe you feel very shy inside, but manage to hide the shyness and appear to be comfortable. Maybe you're outgoing with your friends and immediate family, but shy with strangers or in unfamiliar situations. Maybe sometimes, like at school on a regular day or at the beach with friends, you're not shy at all. But at a school dance or at a party with some people you don't know well, you're suddenly feeling tongue-tied.

If any of this sounds like you, relax. You have lots of company. Most people—of all ages—report that shyness is or has been a problem for them at times.

Why are people shy?

Psychologists have a lot of different ideas about this. Some say that many people are shy because they are self-centered: They are so caught up in thinking about themselves and worrying about what other people think of them that they can't relate to other people easily. Others contend that shyness can start with a poor self-image which, in turn, can come from past experiences: maybe you were teased a lot by classmates about a physical trait like being skinny or fat or short or wearing glasses, and/or you came from a home where so much was expected of you that you're now terrified of making a mistake or failing at anything.

Some researchers are finding that shyness *may* be an inborn trait—that some people are just naturally shy.

Whether you were born shy or became shy as the result of the way people have treated you or the way you've come to see yourself, you *can* change. You're *not* doomed to stand on the sidelines feeling uncomfortable for the rest of your life! While you may always feel a *little* shy at times, there is a lot you can do to feel more comfortable with others.

These are just a few ways to get started:

Don't Label—Or Mislabel—Yourself As an Impossibly Shy Person. Labels don't help. They just restrict you to acting a certain way and give you that hopeless feeling, "I can't change because this is just the way I am." Also, labels can be wrong. Maybe you're not truly shy, but simply quiet. Or maybe you're just shy in some situations. Instead of telling yourself, "I'm shy and there's nothing I can do about it!" *ask* yourself, "When do I feel shy? What situations or which people make me feel shy? When do I do pretty well with others? And what's the difference between these times and these people—and the times when I'm shy?"

When you know exactly when shyness is a problem for you and when it isn't, then you can make a plan of action to help you through the tough times.

Stop Expecting So Much of Yourself. If you're like a lot of shy people, you see a very thin line between success and total failure: If you can't be the life of the party, then you're a total social failure. If people don't warm up to you immediately, you're convinced they hate you.

With expectations like these, no wonder you feel intimidated. The fact is, almost no one can consistently be the life of the party, the center of attention, instantly accepted or liked by everyone. Even the most popular people you know aren't always in top form or liked by everyone. And it usually takes other people *time* to get to know, accept, and like you. This is especially important to remember when you're starting a new school and other people seem to be mostly indifferent. It could be they're feeling shy with you! And even if they're not, they need time to get to know you in order to see if a close and lasting friendship is possible.

The difference between a shy person and someone who doesn't suffer from shyness is often that this second person doesn't have such high expectations, so when something doesn't turn out just right, he or she doesn't have so far to fall. People who aren't shy don't tend to agonize over a wrong answer in class or a joke that fell flat, or an embarrassing silence in the middle of a conversation. That person will think, "How embarrassing! But I'll survive!" or "Well, I can't win or be right all the time even though I wish I could."

Try giving yourself the same realistic expectations. Sometimes you'll make a friend and sometimes you won't. You can't always say exactly the right thing. Everyone has embarrassing experiences. But it's a lot less painful to accept these as part of life—not life-ruining—to calm down and go on, and maybe even laugh about it later.

This is all easy to say and hard to do . . . but ask yourself what's the very worst that could happen in any situation—and tell yourself that, whatever happens, you'll survive.

Take Small Steps Toward Change. If you try to change your whole outlook on life and your personality, particularly in a very short time, you're putting yet another incredible expectation on yourself! Too much change all at once can be overwhelming. Start slow and build on each success.

People who are struggling to overcome serious problems with drinking, drugs, or other compulsive behavior are often advised to change some aspect of their behavior "Just for today . . ." That strategy can work for *you,* too.

For example, you might tell yourself "Just for today . . . I'll say 'Hi' to one new person."

Or you might say, "Just for today, I'll start a conversation with someone I really like, but don't know well. I won't try for brilliant. I won't try for long. I'll just exchange a few pleasant words with someone I'd like to know better."

No matter how the other person reacts, whether he or she says "Hi" back or enthusiastically joins the conversation, you're still a winner because you did what you decided to do . . . just for today. You aren't responsible for other people's moods, manners, and choices. You can only be in charge of your own. And if you can accomplish what you decided to do just for today, you're taking another successful step away from shyness.

Become Aware of Subtle, Quiet Ways You May Be Keeping Others From Getting to Know You. When you talk or are simply with a group of people, do you make eye contact? Do you smile? Do you lean toward them to hear what they have to say? Or do you look away with your arms folded protectively across your chest?

You may know that you don't make eye contact or treat others with physical openness and warmth because you're scared of rejection and shy. But others don't always know that. They may assume that you're stuck-up, or that you don't like them or aren't interested in what they have to say.

Do you get upset when you say "Hi" to people, but they never answer back? Does it seem like everyone, even people who are usually pretty nice and friendly to others, is ignoring you? Maybe they can't hear you. Maybe you're speaking so softly or speaking without looking at them—and they don't realize you're greeting *them*! Try, just for today, saying "Hi" to someone in a firm, clear voice, look at that person and smile—as if you weren't shy at all. You may be surprised at the difference!

This doesn't mean that you have to change your whole personality. It's okay to be quiet and reserved if that's your nature and you're happy being that way. But, to be content, you need to have a real choice between being quiet and speaking up when you need and want to.

You can conquer shyness without trying to become someone you're not. The ideal step from shyness is not aggressiveness, but comfort and joy in being with others. You can do that in a quiet way if that's the way you are.

You may have heard the Aesop fable about the contest between the wind and the sun and which was more powerful. It has a useful message for shy people.

It seems that the wind and the sun noticed a traveler walking along a road and argued which one of them could make the traveler remove his coat first. The wind blew furiously, but this only made the traveler wrap his coat more tightly around himself. But when the sun shone warmly on him, he quickly removed the coat. The point of this fable is that people who push too hard, who are too phony or *on,* too focused on getting people to like them, may push people away, causing them to wrap themselves more tightly in themselves or in their own pre-existing circle of friends. But genuine warmth, whether it is expressed quietly or with talk and laughter, seems to get through to most people. You can express warmth without saying a lot—or anything. You can show you care by listening with interest, by really looking at and paying attention to another person. You can show warmth with a touch, with a smile, with a cheerful greeting, by remembering and asking about something that is important to another. There are many ways that you can take the risk of showing someone you care and that you want to be friends—and many ways you can succeed, if you bring warmth into your words or actions.

Selectively Share Your Feelings With Others. One of the most painful aspects of feeling shy is feeling all alone—feeling that everyone else is perfectly confident. But that's not true! Most people, especially young people, feel shy at times. And with people you like a lot, people who seem sensitive to others' feelings, you might try admitting that you feel shy. They may reassure you or, at least, let you know that you're not alone by admitting that they feel shy sometimes, too. And sharing feelings like that can help to build a very special friendship.

Mike is a quiet, somewhat shy person, who had always felt awkward when trying to talk with a girl on the phone, at a party—anywhere! "I always thought I had to try to be cool and I just couldn't bring it off," he says. "I thought if I ever admitted to a girl that I was shy, she'd think I was a real dork. Probably some girls would. But when I went out with Penny the first time, I told her that I was kind of nervous because I'm shy. I just had a feeling she'd understand. And she did! She smiled, looked relieved and said, 'I thought *I* was the only shy and nervous person here!' And we got along really well from then on. We like each other a lot!"

Sharing your feelings with someone you think will understand can help you to feel less different and much less alone.

LONELINESS

Please help me. I feel so alone. It's like no one cares about me. I don't have any real friends. I don't have a boyfriend, even though I'm in ninth grade and most of my friends are dating. I mostly sit at home feeling sorry for myself. Is this the way it's always going to be for me?? Help!!

Nicole Y.

Why is it that some people don't have friends even though they try to be friendly? I'm not shy. I tell people what I feel about things. I joke around. But nobody is friends with me. I'm not ugly, and like I said, I try to be friendly and say "Hi" to everyone. So what's wrong? Why am I feeling lonely and friendless when I'm not doing anything wrong?

"Confused"

We've all felt lonely at times. Maybe it was when a best friend moved away or a love relationship broke up. Maybe it was when there were family problems we couldn't understand—parents divorcing or fighting, a sick or troubled brother or sister needing a lot of attention. Maybe it was when a favorite pet died or got lost. Maybe it was the time we started a new school and saw only strangers' faces—and felt absolutely invisible.

Loneliness doesn't just happen to constantly lonely people. It happens to every-one, especially in the early teen years when it's so easy to feel different from others and to feel all alone, when friends and classmates aren't always *consistently* nice and you may not feel as close to your parents as you used to be.

It can feel lonely when, like Nicole, you compare yourself to others and wonder why you don't have a special boyfriend or girlfriend in your life, why everyone else seems to be a success at dating and you haven't really even started.

And you can feel painfully lonely when, like "Confused," you really *try* to get close to others, but all your efforts fail and you don't know why.

For some people, loneliness is situational: they miss a friend, they long for a date or wish they had a special person to eat lunch with. When that situation changes, they're not lonely anymore.

But for other people, it isn't quite that simple. For some people, loneliness is a habit, a way of life, a trap they can't quite escape. Sometimes this happens because they don't make an effort to change the circumstances that are helping to make them lonely—like watching TV night after night instead of getting involved in activities and interests where they're likely to meet potential friends. Sometimes people end up lonely because they do things, without realizing it, that turn other people off.

Recently, some psychologists did a study of a group of people who said they were usually lonely and another group who were not lonely. They were put in a party setting and observed. The psychologists found that the lonely people talked more about themselves and showed less interest in others. They didn't ask questions. And so they missed yet another opportunity to get to know another person. Some lonely people don't realize that the best way to get someone interested in you is to be interested in them.

Some lonely people also don't realize that other people need time to get to know you. If you rush in, touching another person a lot and telling him or her *everything* about yourself all at once, he or she is likely to feel overwhelmed and put off, maybe a little embarrassed.

This isn't meant to blame someone who is lonely and unhappy. No one purposely wants to turn others off. No one wants to be lonely.

Of course, there *are* people who like being alone. That's different. Being alone is not the same as being lonely. In fact, learning to enjoy your own company, finding happiness in being alone sometimes as well as sharing good times with others, is a very important part of becoming a mature person.

How can you start enjoying time alone and begin to beat loneliness?

Find Ways to Feel Better About Yourself. People who are lonely a lot quite often don't like themselves much and don't consider themselves good company.

When you feel bad about yourself, you're likely to assume that other people feel the same way about you. You're likely to anticipate rejection—and so will often avoid that possibility by keeping to yourself.

You may also dread moments alone with yourself because you find yourself boring to be with, or because being alone at times just confirms your sense of being a total failure.

These painful feelings can create nonstop misery for you unless you begin to replace them with positive feelings and good experiences.

Think of hobbies or activities that help you to feel a sense of accomplishment and try these again, even if it has been awhile.

Learn something new you've always wanted to learn. For Jill, this meant asking her grandmother to teach her some handicraft skills. For Brad, it meant trying cross-country skiing for the first time at a Y outing.

Make a list of your good qualities as a step toward learning to appreciate your own company. If you have trouble coming up with any for your list, ask someone for some ideas.

Treat yourself nicely—like a dear friend—and you'll feel more like being one for yourself. Instead of saying to yourself, "Well, see, you're a real nobody because here it is Saturday night and you're home alone—again!" you might say instead: "Now I have some time for myself to do something *I* really enjoy!"

And then *do* whatever it is that you enjoy!

Make the Most of Your Alone Time. If you spend your time alone just watching TV or staring at the ceiling feeling sorry for yourself or rejecting any ideas for fun just because you don't have a companion at the moment, no wonder you hate being alone!

Make a list of fun things to do by yourself—and then do them!

- Write in your diary.
- Read something just for fun.
- Exercise.
- Listen to your favorite music and sing along.
- Take a long walk and notice all the beautiful or interesting sights along the way.
- Get involved in volunteer work or some other group activities. This can be a good way to feel better about yourself, learn something new, and meet people—all at the same time!
- Write letters to a pen pal or a friend who has moved away.
- Go to the library and check out a book on a subject that has sparked your curiosity, but one that you know little, if anything, about. You may have the joy of finding a brand-new interest!
- Take pleasure in the season: Let yourself get excited (as you used to be as a child) about the first snowfall, and then romp in the snow with your dog; feel the autumn leaves crunch underfoot and the crisp breeze on your cheeks as you enjoy the spectacular fall colors; take a walk after an early spring rain, enjoy the fresh, clean air, and look for the first signs of spring flowers; sit outside on a balmy summer evening and watch the stars start to appear, count fireflies, and try to identify all the wonderful sounds of the night. It's hard to feel truly alone when you're busy enjoying the special wonders all around you.

There may be times when you think, "But a beautiful sight—the first snow or a spectacular sunset or a blaze of autumn color—really isn't special unless I am sharing it with someone."

It's true that sharing a wonderful sight or experience with someone else can be one of the great joys of life.

But *you* are someone special, too! Solitary pleasures are no less beautiful or real than pleasures shared with another. All the fun, beauty, and excitement of new discoveries and treasured memories are a part of you, whether you experience these alone or with someone else you like—or love—a lot.

Take the Risk of Reaching Out to Others. Get involved with other people. Start greeting them first, asking questions, giving sincere compliments, remembering a birthday with warm good wishes, pursuing activities where you can meet other people with similar interests. Let other people know you: what you believe, how you feel, what you enjoy. With some you especially like and trust, share some of your dreams, your uncertainties and your fears. You may realize that you're not alone, that other people feel the same way you do. When you take the risk of being open with another, you may make it easier for someone to do the same with you.

Of course, there may be times when things don't work out the way you had hoped. You open your heart to another and get ridiculed or rejected. That can hurt a lot.

But it's still worth the risk. If you keep to yourself and never try to let others know you, nothing will happen. You'll just go on being lonely. When you reach out, something wonderful could happen. If you're rejected, you'll feel hurt, of course, but you'll survive. If you don't take the risk of being close to others, you may never know the joy of feeling accepted by and being close to another person.

Being close to another isn't nonstop joy, of course. There are times of pleasure and times of pain, times when you laugh and share your feelings easily, and times when you don't understand each other and feel, suddenly, very alone again. But when you're in touch with others—whether it's a joyful time or a difficult time—you'll leave behind that empty, on-the-outside-forever feeling of loneliness.

STRESS

Lately I've been feeling under a lot of pressure. I just started middle school and it scares me. I wonder if I'll ever have any close friends with so many strangers all around me. I keep forgetting the combination of my locker and it makes me late to class and then I get in trouble. My parents are already going on about how my grades have to be perfect so I can get into college. And the first dance of the year is next week, and I'm scared about going and having everyone ignore me and not being asked to dance. Everything is harder now. Homework is harder. My parents expect me to act more adult and take care of my little sister and brother a lot more. I'm tired a lot and it's hard to get used to my body being different, even though I'm happy about most of the changes. What's going on with me—and how can I start feeling better?

Hilary J.

Is it normal to feel nervous and upset about other people's problems? My parents are fighting a lot because my dad lost his job and hasn't been able to get another one yet. There are some real money problems. I'd almost rather be at school than at home because of the fighting. But school isn't easy, either. I'm shorter than most of the other guys and get teased a lot. Every girl I see is taller than me and they don't want to dance with me at school dances. My grades are okay, but everyone says they could be better. It's just that it's hard to concentrate on homework a lot when I worry so much.

John W.

Stress is a part of all our lives. It is especially likely to happen when you're experiencing changes—either happy or upsetting changes.

You may be feeling a lot of stress now if:

• You're experiencing—or facing—a change in schools.
• Your physical development is behind or ahead that of most of your classmates.

- There are problems at home: parents fighting, an alcoholic parent, a serious illness in the family, money worries, a parental separation or divorce, psychological or physical abuse from a parent or sibling.
- Someone close to you died in the past year—a grandparent, parent or other close relative, a special friend, or a pet.
- Everyone in your life seems to expect a lot of you now—from the coach at P.E. to all your teachers and your parents.
- You're feeling a lot of conflicting things: sometimes loving and sometimes feeling close to hating your parents; wanting to be on your own, but sometimes secretly wishing you could be a little kid and totally taken care of again; feeling close to, yet competitive with, a good friend; wanting to be a good person, but feeling that, lots of times, you fall short.

When you're under stress, you may start feeling overwhelmed: You have too much to do in too little time, you can't possibly do everything you feel you must do. You may feel angry, unfairly judged, and impatient with yourself and others. You may feel you don't have enough time to have fun or to be with the people you most enjoy. You may cry and get upset about small things. You may worry about *everything*!

Some people live with stress by just accepting it and spend a lifetime racing the clock and feeling overwhelmed. Some people try to calm their feelings with alcohol or drugs or food. Others refuse to face any stress—which can also be part of growth and opportunity—and so, in a very real sense, drop out of life and spend their time being bored and unfulfilled.

There *are* better ways to cope with stress!

While you can't completely avoid stress, you *can* take control of your life and make it less painful.

Put Yourself in Control. While you can't control everything that goes on in your life (you still have to go to school, take exams and things like that), you *can* feel more in control. You can start by taking responsibility for feelings of nervousness, anxiety, and stress in certain situations. For example, you may have always told yourself, "Strangers make me nervous." If you can say, instead, "I get nervous when I'm with strangers," you are in control and can choose to change your behavior or certain nerve-wracking situations.

Take control of the amount of stress in your life. If you're going through a tough time at school, don't look for more stress by getting into fights with your parents. If you're starting a new school in the fall, try to take summer classes there or join a youth group attended by other people at your new school so you will know at least *some* people there before school starts. If you find yourself feeling overwhelmed, slow down. Eliminate unnecessary pressures, activities, or relationships that leave you feeling that it's all just too much. (Who needs a bossy, critical friend when you're busy dealing with teachers and parents who expect a lot of you? Why take up another club or hobby that doesn't interest you that much when you're already feeling you have no time to relax or to just be with friends?)

When you begin to take control and to make decisions about risks, interests, and activities you will and won't pursue, you'll start feeling better.

Keep Your Day-to-Day Life Fairly Simple and Predictable. With so many changes going on in your life—your changing body, your social and academic changes, your evolving relationship with your parents—a simple daily routine can be a relief! Familiar things you can look forward to and things that you just do without it having to be a big decision can be soothing. Go to bed and get up at set times. Decide—and stick to—a regular study schedule. Eat regular, well-balanced meals. And leave some time in every day for fun!

Make Time for Fun. It's important for your emotional and physical health to have fun every day. Making time for exercise you enjoy, talking with or writing to someone special, listening to music, meditating, pursuing a special interest or hobby is an *important* part of your day! People who know how to play and who allow themselves to have fun, even for a short time, every day will never spend a lifetime feeling overwhelmed and overburdened.

Use Exercise to Relieve Tension. Exercise is much better at calming you down than any artificial means like drugs or alcohol or Oreos. And, in the process, your body can be stronger and healthier, too! Next time you feel angry, frustrated, or at the end of your patience, take an exercise break! Slip on your roller blades and head out. Take a long walk. Run. Dance to your favorite music. Go hit tennis balls against an outside wall. Put an exercise tape on the VCR and work out. You'll feel better and may be able to go back and face your stressful situation in a much more positive way.

Tell Yourself That a Failure Is Not a Disaster and That You Are Not What You Do. This can be especially useful around exam time when you're biting your nails and saying, "If I don't pass this test, that's IT! I'm finished. My life will never be the same." Or if you don't get a part in a school play or get chosen for a committee you want, you may feel that you've failed totally.

Life isn't like that. You may not get the grade you had hoped. But you can use a disappointment, even a failure, as a learning experience, as a way to do better next time. If you don't get what you want now, you can get it another time. If you make everything a test or a turning point—if you don't pass this test, you'll never go to college, if you don't get a date with this person you'll be miserable, lonely, and unloved for life—it can put a lot of pressure on you and take the joy out of what could be triumphs. Because when you *do* get what you want, you'll be so busy being afraid you'll lose it or won't accomplish your next goal that you'll hardly take time to savor what's happening right now.

It can be a lot less stressful to say to yourself, "I really want to do well. I'm going to do the best I can do—and that's *all* I can do. And if things don't turn out the way I hope they do, it *isn't* the end of the world."

It's also important to separate who you are from what you do.

Feeling that you are being judged as a worthwhile (or not worthwhile person) when a paper is being graded can make you immobilized with fear or you can procrastinate on the paper until it's too late to do the kind of job you want to do. It can take a lot of joy out of what could be a satisfying challenge.

I remember learning this from a very special friend when I was in junior high. Mac, an 88-year-old friend of my family's, was a sort of adopted grandfather for me. One day, he called when I was home alone, struggling over a term paper, worrying about exams and, not so incidentally, wondering if a boy I thought about constantly would ever notice I was alive. Mac asked me how I was. I immediately poured out my worries about school and this boy. Mac listened carefully and with love, asking questions and making some gentle suggestions.

Finally, after I had told him all the problems and fears of my life, he asked me again: "Now, dear, how are *you*?"

I thought for a moment—past all the cares and worries—and said, "Me? Oh, I guess, when you get right down to it, *I'm* fine!"

You are not your grades. You are not your work. You are not your social life. You are valuable as a unique person with a variety of strengths, weaknesses, feelings, and ideas. You are so much more than you do or achieve. These achievements may give you some satisfaction, but that's all. The most special thing about you, whether you win top grades, prizes, have a date or not, is that you are special just because you exist. There has never been and there will never be anyone exactly like you. Feeling joy in just being yourself and being alive can make all the challenges of your life less scary and the successes you do have much more fun!

Talk to Others. When you're feeling stress and worry, it can help to talk to someone about it. You'll feel less alone. It can be a relief to talk. Maybe the other person will have some good suggestions. Or maybe you'll find a new solution to your problem while you're talking with someone else about it.

Take an Imaginary Vacation. Take a few moments, relax, close your eyes, and go back to a place you find peaceful and pleasant. Maybe you'll imagine yourself on a sunny beach or in a beautiful garden or walking through a forest. Maybe you'll imagine yourself lying in a hammock on your grandparents' porch on a summer night, gently swinging and listening to the crickets. Maybe you'll imagine yourself lying in the grass, looking up at the clouds as if you had all the time—and not a care—in the world.

Taking this little vacation in your mind can be a real stress reliever. And you can do it just about any time you want!

BOREDOM

I'm so bored, I can't stand it! I live in this horrible town where there's nothing to do. I'm just 13, so I can't drive somewhere else. All I can do is sit around feeling bored. Everyone I know is bored, too. I can't get out of here for years yet. How can I keep myself from dying of boredom?

Paul H.

How do you know if you're boring? I'm bored a lot but that's because I don't have a lot of friends. I was wondering if I look boring to other people and if that's why I'm alone and bored. If I were out with other people, it would be different. Both my parents work and so I'm home alone a lot, watching TV and just thinking how boring life is. Will it always be this way?

Megan M.

Psychologist Sol Gordon is fond of saying, "When you're bored, you're boring!" And that does have a real ring of truth to it. When you're bored, you're immobilized. You're stuck. You're not interested in anything. You don't feel like doing anything. You sit around waiting for something to happen instead of making something happen. You lack the confidence to try something new. You may have decided that your town or your family or your life in general is just so impossibly boring that you can't do anything to change this. You may be trying to keep from feeling or facing painful facts or feelings in your life, so you numb yourself to everything—joy as well as pain. Boredom can be a part of or can lead to depression.

So how do you know if you may be bored—or boring?

Some warning signs:

- You have no interests.
- You look to others to make life fun and interesting for you.
- You watch TV for hours every day.
- You never ask anyone to do anything with you. You sit around and stare at your toes, feeling bored and waiting to be asked out.
- You complain a lot—about everything and everybody.
- You're never serious.
- You're always serious—and have no sense of humor.
- You're critical and sarcastic—keeping others at a safe distance.
- You act like a know-it-all and are too busy talking to listen and learn; too busy spreading rumors to get to know anyone really well; too busy bragging about things you have (or haven't) done to share in the successes and joys of others.
- You assume that your stories, your jokes, your vacation pictures, your poems are totally fascinating—and worthy of an unlimited amount of someone else's time.
- You impose private feelings or problems on people: you get stoned and sit at a friend's party just giggling and muttering to yourself; you drink too much and throw up (this is especially boring—and boorish—if you do it in someone's car or anywhere in a house except the bathroom); you insist on talking endlessly about sexual feelings and experiences. (Dr. Gordon contends that one of the most super-boring things you can do is to go around telling people you're horny.)

We all have moments when we're bored—and maybe in danger of being boring. But if boredom is fast becoming a way of life for you and you have more than a sneaking suspicion that people's eyes are starting to glaze over with boredom at the mere sight of you, there *are* things you can do to escape from this very tiring cycle of boredom.

If Everything Seems Boring, Try to Think of the Least Boring Activity You Know and Then Do It. This is another thought from Sol Gordon—and it works! What matters is that you start breaking the boring cycle of inactivity.

Learn Something New Today. Read a newspaper or magazine you wouldn't ordinarily read. Go to a museum. Listen to a different kind of music. Talk with someone new and ask lots of questions. Try writing a poem or a song. Dust off the encyclopedia and look through a section you've never read before. Or go to the dictionary and learn one new word every day. If you keep your mind active, you'll never be constantly bored—or boring!

Realize That Growing Up Doesn't Mean Leaving All Your Childhood Loves, Interests, and Enthusiasm Behind. All of us, whatever our ages, are a combination of our earlier selves. We always carry with us the child we once were. When you're not far away from being a child, that may seem threatening and you try to deny that part of yourself because you think it means being immature.

But just because you're growing up doesn't mean you can't be spontaneous, show joy and curiosity and enthusiasm. That's not being immature. That's part of being a complete, happy, *alive* person. Being open to ideas and to pleasures, both old and new, can keep you growing—and *not* bored—throughout your life.

Think of All the Things You Enjoy Or Used to Enjoy. When you let pleasure into your life, there's very little room for boredom. Think about hobbies or interests you used to enjoy. Try one or more of these again. Think about special things or special people who bring joy to your life. When you really stop to think about it, what makes you glad to be alive?

For Kerry, a formerly bored 14-year-old, her pleasure list includes: "My cat Freddie (I love burying my face in his white stomach fur and listening to him purr); taking a walk early in the morning and watching the changing colors in the sky; country-western music for a change once in a while; talking with my friends Mary and Jen; going to the mall just to people-watch; those rare times when my mom listens to my opinions and says, 'You're right!'; soft sweaters, especially if they're blue or gray; being in the house all alone and singing or playing the stereo as loud as I want; Christmas Eve (especially if it's snowing); being young enough to have lots of dreams for the future (like falling in love and moving somewhere interesting, traveling, having my own car and apartment, a life of my own!)."

What would *you* include on your list of past, present, and future pleasures?

Do Something Nice for Someone. This can break up the routine of your life, make someone else happy, and help you to feel better about yourself:

• This can mean saying "Hi" to someone you usually ignore;
• Apologizing to someone you've hurt;
• Rediscovering a friendship you've neglected—and this can be nice for *you* as well as your friend!;
• Running an errand for a sick or elderly relative or neighbor, or helping with his or her yardwork *without* expecting payment;
• Doing volunteer work at your church, library, hospital, nursing home, or other social service agency;
• Teaching someone who is struggling with a skill: helping a friend who is having study problems, helping your younger sister learn how to dance, taking time to help a foreign-born classmate learn English, helping a friend to organize her room so she can *find* stuff;
• Making someone else's life a little easier. Offer to watch younger siblings so your mom can have an afternoon or evening to do whatever she wants. Rake leaves *before* your dad asks you—just to surprise him. Spend some time listening to an old person's stories of the past. You *might* actually find these interesting—and it might also mean a lot to the older person to share something of his or her past with you.

When you're involved with others in such positive ways, you'll feel a *part* of life in a new way. You'll be amazed at how many people, subjects, and things interest you—and how rarely you are ever bored!

DEPRESSION

What can you do if you've lost hope of life ever being better? I can hardly get out of bed in the morning (and sometimes I don't) because I feel so down and like there's no way I can change anything. Sometimes I think I'd rather be dead, but I haven't thought of a way of suicide that doesn't scare me yet. Please help me!

Lynette J.

I feel bad because my parents are getting divorced and my dad is marrying someone else and they're moving to another state, so I probably won't see him much anymore. Also, my mom has to move, too, and I'm going to be changing schools right in the middle of eighth grade. This is the worst because I was just starting to feel really good about having a good bunch of friends at my old school. What can I do to feel better? I feel so low I can't think of anything.

Jim K.

Depression can be a major problem for people of all ages, but it can be particularly painful for you right now.

Why? There are several reasons. First, depression is an emotional response to loss and change in your life. You're going through a lot of changes right now—and along with these, some real losses.

For example, in growing up, you lose a familiar way of looking and being (even if you're mostly glad to be looking more grown up). In going to middle school or junior high, you lose the status of part of the most mature and smartest class in elementary school. You may fall in love—and lose that love—for the first time. You may feel newly independent, but feel the loss, at times, of being able to depend on your parents for everything. And, as you try to be more independent, you may keep your feelings inside more, not sharing them with the parent or other adult you used to talk with all the time. And that can be a loss. So you're experiencing, because of your stage of life, more changes and losses than most people.

Second, you're not used to dealing with losses. That's why losing a first love hurts so very much . . . so much you think you'll never get over it. That's why going to a large junior high where you don't know a lot of people can be so frightening. (It may be hard to remember how frightened you were when you started your now familiar elementary school as a little kindergartner or first grader!) At a time when you're dealing with so much change, you're also having to learn how to cope with all this and discovering, little by little, that no matter how scary a situation or how great a loss you experience, you will survive. This learning doesn't always keep up conveniently with your losses, and there may well be times when you feel you *can't* stop hurting, when you will never feel better, when a situation seems truly hopeless.

There are different types of depression. It can be brief—or last a long time. Depression may be tied to a specific loss like a romantic breakup or the death of a pet or not making a team. This is very painful, but gradually, as you talk, cry, write in your diary, and generally work through your feelings, you begin to feel better and within a matter of days or a few weeks, you're starting to recover. You may feel the pain for a long time, but it doesn't keep you from leading your normal, everyday life.

Prolonged depression, which some experts call a significant depression, is slower to develop, sometimes difficult to identify, and can interfere a great deal with your life.

A noted psychiatrist, Dr. Helen DeRosis, says: "With a significant depression, you may feel, at first, that you're inferior and helpless to change your situation. You may feel intense anger, guilt, self-hate, and hopelessness. When you try to keep these strong feelings inside yourself (keeping them *depressed*) *you* become depressed and feel totally numb."

Knowing when you're depressed isn't always easy. Some depressed teens don't *act* draggy, down, and depressed. They may act angry and get into fights at school. Or they may have a lot of physical symptoms like headaches and stomach-aches.

How do you know if you may be depressed?

The more "Yes" answers you have to the following questions, the more likely it is that you are feeling depressed.

- Do you dread getting up in the morning? (This is especially significant if you *used* to be a morning person and always used to look forward to starting a new day.)
- Do you have trouble sleeping at night—and spend a lot of time thinking dark thoughts, pacing, or crying?
- Are you always tired—even if you have had plenty of sleep?
- Have you lost your appetite and find that you are unable to eat or have no interest in eating most meals?
- Have you started eating everything in sight, even when you're not hungry and especially when you're feeling angry, sad, frustrated, or bored?
- Have you lost interest in everything—even things you used to enjoy?
- Are you having trouble concentrating?
- Are your grades going down?
- Are you suddenly having other problems at school—getting into fights, skipping classes or unable to bring yourself to go to school at all?
- Have you stopped caring how you look?
- Do you feel that doing *anything* (even phoning a friend) is more trouble than it's worth?
- Do you have trouble making decisions—even small ones?
- Do you feel that nothing you do will ever make any difference—in your own life or in the world in general?
- Do you get unusually upset or angry lately about little things that never used to bother you?
- Do you suffer a lot from headaches, stomachaches, or constipation?
- Have you given up the idea of talking to anyone about your feelings because you're sure no one would understand—or you aren't really sure *how* you feel, just that you feel bad?

- Do you see the future as hopeless and unchangeable?
- Have you found yourself crying a lot without knowing why? Or are you unable to cry—feeling *beyond* tears?
- Have you thought of taking your own life?

A word of caution: When you're in your early teens and going through all the hormonal, physical, and social changes, there are times when your feelings will be very up and down and unpredictable. You may feel tired. You may not feel as close to the people you love or enjoy quite the same things you used to enjoy as a child. All of these can simply be a part of your growth process.

But if you have had a lot of "Yes" answers and feel that your life is hopeless and there's nothing you can do about it, you could well be depressed.

There are a number of ways you can help yourself.

Force Yourself to Do One Thing Different Today. Instead of oversleeping, get up and get dressed. If you've been dragging around in old jeans with barely combed hair, take extra care with your grooming today and wear something that looks great on you! If you've been a social hermit, take a deep breath, then call a friend. Or simply ask yourself, "What would I do right now if I weren't depressed?" Then *do* it! Sometimes when you stop *acting* so depressed, this can be the first step away from feeling so depressed.

Find Ways to Express Those Depressed Feelings Without Hurting Yourself Or Someone Else. Write an angry letter to someone, read it over, and then tear it up. Cry. Pound your pillows. Or go running. Talk to a friend or family member. Start a diary to explore your painful—and not so painful—feelings. Try talking a problem over with someone who seems to be causing one for you, without making angry accusations, just reporting your feelings. Get rid of some of your pent-up anger with a game of tennis or racquetball. Or take a long walk or bike ride.

Resist the Drug Or Alcohol Cure. Some people use drugs or alcohol to try to get rid of painful feelings, including depression. But these substances only make depression worse. They can also postpone any solutions to your problems—and can also add to these problems. Who needs more problems? Besides, learning to face and deal with feelings and problems is a way to grow up to be strong and independent.

Get Daily Exercise. No matter how tired or down or sick you feel, do *something* to give your body a workout every day. It doesn't have to be a long, elaborate workout. Just take a walk. Ride your bike. Jump rope. Swim. Do sit-ups. Even if it's just a few minutes a day, any kind of exercise can help. Some doctors are finding that exercise can improve your moods and can be especially helpful in fighting depression. This may be because people who exercise regularly have a larger amount of a pain-fighting, mood-elevating hormone in their bodies. It may also be because, once you start moving or get out and see a bit of the world, you won't feel life is quite so unchangeable or hopeless.

Give Yourself Something to Look Forward to Every Day. It doesn't have to be a big treat or event, just something you enjoy. Take a hot bath or shower. Listen to a favorite *upbeat* song. Re-read a poem that means a lot to you or a letter from a special person that made you feel especially good when you first received it—and whenever you re-read it. Visit a favorite place and just sit there taking in the sights and sounds for a while. Talk with someone who helps you to laugh or to see your good qualities. Hug someone special. The closeness will feel good to *you*, too.

If You're Feeling Too Overwhelmed by Depression to Help Yourself Or Are Thinking of Suicide, Seek Help from Others Right Away! People feel hopeless and totally overwhelmed when they don't see the possibility for change. Most people with suicidal feelings don't really want to die—they just want life to be different, but don't know how to make it different.

Only death makes growth and change impossible. It's important to remember one thing when you're feeling helpless and hopeless in your depression: AS LONG AS THERE IS LIFE, THERE IS HOPE.

And other people who care can help you to find that hope. These other people can be friends who help you to feel loved and accepted. But if you're feeling this depressed, this hopeless, you also need help from some adults.

Tell your parents how you're feeling and ask for help. Most parents care deeply, despite everyday criticisms or nagging, and will do anything possible to help if they realize you're in real trouble. But if your parents *don't* help you, go to a teacher or the parent of a friend or another adult relative. Tell your family doctor or a clergyperson how you feel.

If you're feeling suicidal and don't feel you can talk to anyone you know, call a Suicide Prevention Hotline or a crisis line in your area (check the white pages of your phone book for the Suicide Prevention Hotline or "Crisis Prevention Hotline"). If you keep reaching out, someone will be there.

No matter how terrible your situation, how hopeless it may all seem, there *is* hope for the future. Sometimes opening up to a parent or other family member will help bring about needed changes. Sometimes finding support from others will help you to live through a very painful, temporarily unchangeable situation until time changes the event. (Even if you're stuck with a parent or stepparent you can't stand, there *is* hope! In a few years, you'll be grown up and independent and can leave. Go to school. Learn job skills. Get ready to be independent as soon as you can.) And if you're depressed because of a serious abuse problem at home, tell another adult and let him or her help you. You don't have to live with danger or terrible abuse. There *are* alternatives.

People do care and will help you, even if that seems unlikely at the moment. You are not unloved. You are not alone. Reach out and you'll see. No situation is truly hopeless—as long as you are alive.

LIVING WITH CHANGING FEELINGS

I used to look up to adults, including my parents, but now they're making me mad! I hate it when they think they're always right just because they're older. I hate it when my parents make plans for us to take a vacation at our grandparents' place (AGAIN!) without asking me what I'd like to do. I hate it when people treat me like a baby when I'm almost 13. I can't stand it when some adult says, "You'll understand when you're older . . ." I never used to mind all this, but now I feel different. I get really upset! How can I make them understand?

Kim L.

I'm sure I must be a bad person for doing this, but I think about sex pretty often. I'm not even dating, but I sometimes think about what it would be like to kiss someone passionately or to actually have sex with him. I don't plan to do anything like this for a long time. I'm 12 and my parents won't even let me go out alone with a boy until I'm 16. But I still think about sex. Does this mean something is wrong with me? How can I stop?

S.A.

Changing feelings are, at times, unsettling and, at all times, quite normal.

It's normal to look at the world a bit differently now that you're growing up so fast.

It's understandable to feel angry when you feel so able to do things for yourself and understand things you never could grasp before and yet adults treat you like a child.

Sexual feelings, newly urgent in the early teen years, are entirely normal, too. It isn't bad to have such feelings. They're simply a part of you—like all your other feelings, desires, and sensations. What matters is what you choose to do—or not do—about them.

These changing feelings can give you a great opportunity to try out some of your new insights and maturity as a growing young adult. Just as you're beginning to see adults in a new way, try approaching them in a new way.

For example, if you usually hate your family vacations or can't bear the thought of being trundled off to camp again this summer, bring up the subject well in advance before plans are firmly set. Don't yell, scream, cry, or sulk. Just report your feelings and have some alternatives in mind. You might say, "I'd prefer not to go to camp this year. I'd rather stay home so I can be with my friends more and also take a drama workshop this summer. What do you think about that idea?" Or, if a trip to Grandma's looks inevitable, don't dig in your heels and sullenly refuse to go. Instead, think of a little side trip—to a place near or on the way to or from Grandma's—that all of you might enjoy visiting, and suggest taking a few days to go there before or after the annual visit to Grandma. Your parents might be receptive to that.

When your opinions differ from an adult's, don't preface your remarks with, "You're wrong! I totally disagree . . ." Nothing will make an adult's mind snap shut faster than that! Instead, listen carefully to what he or she has to say. Tell the adult something like, "I understand how you might feel that way and I respect your feelings. Mine are a little different. What I feel is . . ." If you express your differences in a quiet, respectful way—after having listened to the adult—he or she will be more likely to listen to you.

Also, don't assume that, if someone says, "Someday you'll understand . . ." that this person is automatically seeing you as a baby. There are some life experiences that are truly unique.

For example, a person of *any* age who has never been married can't truly understand what it's really like to be married until or unless he or she *is* married. Dating someone for a long time is not the same. Living together unmarried is not the same. The commitment of marriage intensifies the love experience in a totally new way.

In the same way, a divorce is different from breaking up with a longtime boyfriend or girlfriend. It may or may not be more or less painful. It's just different.

Having a child of your own is a very different life experience from baby-sitting or enjoying the children of friends or relatives. Someone who has never had a child may guess what it might be like, but will never really understand the intensity of the love and fear and connection until he or she becomes a parent.

Seeing all of this as simply information and not a put-down may help you to feel better. An adult, while he or she may remember being in junior high or being in love for the first time or worrying about body changes or sexual feelings, also can't know exactly how all of these things are for *you* in this somewhat different time.

Maybe the best response, for teen or adult, is to care, to listen, and to express the feeling, "Of course, I can't know or understand exactly what it's like to be you in your situation. But I do care about you and your feelings a lot!"

Your changing feelings can be an important clue to your own growth.

Having your own opinions, not always agreeing with the adults in your life, wanting to do more things for yourself or on your own are all signs of your growing independence.

At the same time, finding yourself wanting to be a little kid again at times, or occasionally feeling unloved because your parents show more physical affection to a younger brother or sister, may be a sign that you're not quite ready to be totally on your own yet, that you still need protection, guidance, and comfort.

Having new interest in sex and sexual feelings, being interested in boys (or girls) instead of considering all of them pests, is another sign that you're growing up. Feeling uncomfortable with them, finding it strange to have sexual feelings or not feeling ready to have sex are all quite normal signs that you're in a growth process— one that can take many years.

It takes time to develop the social skills and confidence to be truly comfortable with someone of the opposite sex, especially if you haven't grown up with siblings or friends of the opposite sex.

It takes time to accept yourself totally as a sexual being, whether or not you choose to have sex—anytime soon or ever.

And knowing when you're ready to have sex and when you're not, when it's right for you and when it's all wrong, is a very important part of growing up. Many people try to skip over this part, thinking that if they have such feelings, they must act on them. But you can accept and enjoy your sexual feelings long before you actually have sex. This sort of self-acceptance, realizing that your feelings and your sexuality are simply a normal part of you, will help you to make mature, responsible choices about your actions—sexual and otherwise.

Pay attention to your changing feelings. You can learn a lot. You can improve your relationship with the adults around you. You can become a better friend. You can help yourself through some difficult times. You can grow toward an even happier tomorrow if you listen to and learn from your feelings today!

CHAPTER TWO

Your Changing Family

I used to look up to my parents, but now they've changed. They embarrass me all the time. My mother talks too loud and drives this car that's so totally gross, I make her let me off two blocks away from school so no one will see it. My dad sits around on weekends watching TV, wearing this old white T-shirt and baggy pants, and he always asks me questions like where I'm going and when I'll be back right in front of my friends! Most of my friends' parents aren't half as embarrassing as that. What can I do? If I don't have my friends over, they won't like me. I can't exactly ask my parents to go hide in the garage when my friends are over. I know right now what they'd say to that! Help!

"Upset" in Indiana

Until recently, I got along really well with both my parents. Now, all we do is fight. We fight about rules like how late I can stay out. We fight about homework and my grades. We fight about my friends and the fact that I'm the only eighth grader I know who isn't allowed to date. We're always fighting about something! Why are they so down on me? What can I do?

Jody Y.

When you're just getting into your teens and dealing with so many changes in your body, in your social life, and at school, your family life may suddenly start changing, too.

These changes may be like the ones "Upset" and Jody mention: you and your parents are starting to fight more or you're finding your parents more embarrassing than admirable these days.

Or you may feel left out when . . . one or both parents seem to favor a much younger brother or sister . . . or when your parents seem to forget you exist as they concentrate on their work, on their own hobbies and interests, or on each other more than you ever remember.

Or you may feel unfairly criticized when . . . your mom blows up over what you think is a major problem, and she starts going on about how this is the best time of your life . . . or when both parents seem suspicious and want to know everything about you, your activities, and your friends . . . or when a younger brother or sister does something wrong, but they hold *you* responsible . . . or when you're doing the best you can in school, but that doesn't seem to be enough for your parents.

Or you may feel suddenly lonely when . . . you realize that a parent has a special problem, like drinking, and there doesn't seem to be anything you can do about it . . . or when your parents are fighting a lot . . . your parents are getting a divorce (just when you need both of them so much!) . . . your single parent is dating and doesn't have time for you anymore . . . you have too many parents, stepsiblings, or half brothers and sisters, all bugging you and telling you what to do, but with all these people in your life, you still don't feel like you belong anywhere.

Sometimes you may wonder, "Why does my family have to be changing so much now when everything *else* in my life is changing, too!"

The answer is: It's all tied together. Some of the conflicts come about *because* you're changing. Your changes may cause you to see and react to your parents in a new way. Or your parents may, indeed, be treating you in a different way now that you're obviously growing up. Or, with your new, growing maturity, you may simply be more aware of family problems and conflicts than you were as a child.

No one can solve family conflicts and problems in five easy points to follow or in a few—or many—pages of a book. Some of these may be resolved as you continue to grow and mature. Some may be resolved by positive action on your part. And some may be with you and your family for a long time to come. The letters and suggestions in this chapter may give you some reassurance in several ways.

First, you're not alone! Most people of junior high age are dealing with many of the same problems and concerns.

Second, there's a lot you can do to change your feelings, your behavior, and your parents' perceptions of you.

Third, if you can't change a family problem or conflict, you *can* change your reactions to it, learning to be your own person, and feeling good about who you are no matter what is happening in your family.

What *is* happening in your family right now? Maybe some of these common problems will sound familiar.

MY PARENTS TREAT ME LIKE A BABY!

My parents won't let me do anything! They say I can't go out with a guy or even call a boy on the phone. I have to be home every night of the week by eight o'clock!!! The worst thing is, they won't let me shave my legs and my legs are unbelievably hairy. Everyone makes fun of me. (I probably wouldn't have a boyfriend even if my parents let me because of this.) People call me "gorilla legs." My mom says I'm too young to shave. (I'm 12.) My dad says leg hair is natural and I should be proud of it!!!! What can I do before I'm a total outcast?

Chloe H.

My mom treats me like a first grader. She still thinks I should do my homework at the kitchen table with her looking over my shoulder and correcting stuff. I want to do my schoolwork up in my room with the radio on. I can concentrate better. Besides, it really makes me mad to have her hanging over my shoulder like she did when I was little. How can I convince her that I can do my own homework all by myself?

David A.

I'm not as developed as most of my friends. We're all 12, but I look about eight! I'm totally flat. Everyone notices. What upsets me is that everyone talks about their periods and everyone wears bras and I feel left out. I asked my mother if I could get a bra, but she said, "No, you don't need one." How can I keep from feeling so out of it?

Lindsay C.

This is a confusing time for everyone.

There may be times when you feel ready for independence and making all your own decisions. Other times, you may act or react the way you did as a child . . . and want your parents to take care of things. You can be grown up and childlike many different times a day. At a time when you're so close to childhood and yet moving toward adulthood, such feelings are normal. It's just hard to know what you want sometimes. And it's hard for your parents to know how to treat you.

While you have been feeling fairly mature for some time now, your parents have a different time perspective. They may look at you and think (or even worse, *say*!), "It seems like only yesterday when he (she) was just a baby in my arms." It takes most parents time to adjust to the fact that you're growing up. To parents, it seems alarmingly sudden. To you, the growth process, and the push toward independence, may seem agonizingly slow. That's why there can be such a difference between the way your parents treat you and the way you'd *like* to be treated.

Perhaps the best way to show your parents that you're NOT a little kid anymore is to handle differences in the most mature way you can: by listening to what they have to say and then talking about your feelings without attacking them, screaming, crying, or stomping out of the room. Sometimes it's hard. Sometimes it's impossible. But it's worth trying.

For example, Chloe might sit down with her parents and discuss what seems to be the most painful of their limitations: not letting her shave her legs. She might tell them that she feels it's time, that everyone at school is making fun of her, and that she feels like an outcast. Her parents might reply, "You're too young . . . You look fine to me . . . The hair will grow back coarse and heavy . . . You're going to be doing this all your life, so why start so soon?"

She might reply: "I know it seems soon for me to be worried about this, but I think I'm developing fast for my age and my leg hair *is* very noticeable to me and it's embarrassing. What can I do about this?"

When she enlists her parents' suggestions, they may be more likely to be reasonable. A parent might suggest bleaching the hair so it isn't so noticeable. Or Chloe might ask about using a cream hair remover or one of those new electric hair removers that takes hair out by the root instead of cutting it off. When her parents realize that she is really concerned about this and is willing to listen to their feelings, they may concede *and* may begin to take note of the fact that she is growing up.

In the same way, David might approach the conflict over homework with his mother by telling her how much her help over the years has meant to him, but now that he is older, he needs to learn to work on his own.

Maybe his mother needs to feel needed in his life—and he can help her to feel involved in other ways: by telling her how things are going in his life, by asking her opinion on small or important matters.

Maybe his mother thinks that he wouldn't do his homework without her encouragement. If this sounds familiar, ask yourself if there's any truth to this. *Will* you work effectively on your own?

If the answer is "Yes," you might say to your parent: "You've always helped me so much in the past. And I feel good about being able to ask for your help now whenever I need it. But I also need to learn to work on my own now that I'm older. I need to learn to discipline myself to sit down and work. I need to figure out some of this work for myself or else I won't learn it properly. I know when I'm grown up I won't be able to turn to you to solve my work problems, so I'm trying to get used to working on my own more now."

Especially if you back up such comments with action, by working on your own and keeping your grades up, your parents are more likely to see that you're mature enough to be responsible for yourself.

If you're not quite ready to work on your own (you daydream or just listen to music in your room and don't quite get to the homework), you might seek a compromise. Think of a subject you're especially interested in or feel confident about. Ask to do *that* homework alone in your room and then, when you feel your concentration lagging, move back to your traditional homework place with some parental supervision. That way, you can work, little by little, toward total homework independence.

Most parents, as long as they know you're doing what you need to be doing, will be willing to give you more responsibility for your work. With most parents working outside the home, free time is at a premium. There are probably a lot of things your parents would rather do most evenings than hang around making sure you're doing your homework.

Most parents, too, are willing to listen and to consider your feelings once they realize how important something is to you. For example, Lindsay's mother may have tossed off, "You don't need a bra!" relying only on physical fact. What Lindsay may need to do is to let her mother know how painful it is to be different. Instead of simply saying, "Everyone else in my class wears a bra!" (this "everyone else" can be a red flag for a parent and a signal to dig in his or her heels even more firmly or to assume that you're exaggerating), Lindsay might say, "I feel upset and alone because I look different from most of the other girls. I look like a kid and most of the other girls look like adults. I know I can't change how fast I grow or when I get my period, but wearing a bra would help me to feel less different. It would mean a lot to me. Maybe I don't need it physically right now, but it's important to me in other ways."

All of this takes more time to say than "Stop treating me like a baby!" but it may help your parents to understand much better that you're *not* a baby or a little kid anymore—and encourage them to stop treating you that way.

MY PARENTS ARE TOTALLY EMBARRASSING!

What is it about getting older that makes people so embarrassing? My parents are both sort of heavy and they wear stupid, embarrassing clothes. They always say the wrong things in front of my friends or to teachers at open house. It's like they don't care who sees them or what people think about them. What can I do about this?

P.G.

I'm scared everyone will hate me because of my mother. She talks too much and says dumb things. When she gets to laughing sometimes, she snorts!! When she does this in front of my friends, I just want to die!! What's really horrible is when she tells me to do stuff—like cleaning my room or doing some chore—right in front of my friends.

Nina K.

How can I convince my parents not to sit with me when we go to the show? It's bad enough to be going to the movies with my parents on a Saturday night, but I can't stand to sit with them with people from school around (some of them with dates!) because everything will think I'm a total dork. It's embarrassing when they make me sit with them.

Peter J.

If you're like most people, you probably thought your parents could do no wrong only a few years ago. But now . . . have they changed or have *you* changed?

Now that you're growing up, you're trying to separate yourself from them, trying to be liked and accepted by others as your own person. At the same time, you're more aware of your parents as human beings who are less than perfect. And you worry that these imperfections will reflect on you and make others dislike you.

So your embarrassment says two things about you: First, you're struggling to see yourself as a separate person and, second, you're feeling insecure about your own good qualities as a friend or potential friend. You may feel that what you have to offer may not override your parents' embarrassing traits or the fact that others may think you're a baby or unnaturally tied to your parents when you go out with them— when it seems everyone else is going out with dates or, at least, with a group of same-age friends.

If it's any consolation, in a few years, when you feel more secure in your separateness and your own special qualities, your parents' quirks, habits, and peculiarities will be much less threatening to you. You might even volunteer to spend an evening with them or do something as a family—and enjoy it.

But what can you do now?

Separate what embarrasses you into two groups: things that you know you can do something about and those that are pretty unchangeable.

For example, Nina may not be able to do much about her mother's snorting laughter (maybe someday in the future, she'll be happy that her mother enjoys laughing and find herself laughing along), but she may be able to talk with her about another embarrassment: the fact that her mother brings up chores and responsibilities in front of her friends.

Her approach might be like this: "Mom, I get really embarrassed when you tell me to do things or remind me of chores in front of my friends. Could you talk about these things when we're alone?"

Her mother might say, "Nina, my problem is that we're rarely alone. Your friends are over here most of the time and when they are, the chores don't get done. Do you have any ideas what we might do about this?"

After thinking for a time, Nina might decide, "Let's make up a schedule for me to do chores and I'll stick to that. Then you won't have to remind me and I won't forget. I'll post it on the inside of my closet door and I promise to remember."

In this way, both Nina and her mother win their points: The chores will get done and Nina won't be embarrassed so often in front of her friends.

The same approach might work if you go to the movies with your parents, but don't want to sit with them. Don't just slip off and ignore them without warning. Before you set foot out the door, share your feelings with them. You might tell them that, right now, being seen as separate and independent is very important to you, especially when you go someplace where you know you'll run into kids from school. Tell your parents that your embarrassment stems not from being ashamed of them, but needing to look like you're a bit more independent that you are.

Some parents may still not understand this, but many—remembering their own junior high years—are likely to be sympathetic. As long as you let them know that you're not rejecting them as people, but are simply rejecting the *appearance* of childhood dependency, they may be able to view your separate seating arrangement with understanding and good humor.

If you're embarrassed by the way a parent dresses, you may or may not be able to make a difference. By the time they reach middle age, people are pretty set in their ways. There is also quite a difference from one parent type to the next. Some look very young and chic while others look lumpy and every minute their age. A lot of this has to do with heredity. Just as teens develop at different rates, individual people age at different rates. Some of that can't be helped. If a parent is putting on weight, you might offer to help with cooking and try to get your family hooked on healthful salads, fruits, and vegetables. You might suggest taking a walk with a parent so you can talk and exercise at the same time. Or tell a parent that you're concerned about his or her health and would like to help him or her get back in shape. Your concern, rather than your criticism, may cause a parent to make some healthful changes.

You and your parent may have very different concepts of what is stylish clothing. Perhaps the best way to encourage your parents to look what *you* consider their best is to compliment them when they do look good, to tell them which clothes you think look especially nice on them.

On the other hand, tears, jeers, and sarcastic remarks are not likely to get your dad out of his favorite Hawaiian shirt or cause your mom to burn her rumpled sweatsuit. Many parents, who dress up for long hours at work, like to relax in comfortable clothes when they're home. Many of them aren't, at this stage in their lives, so concerned with looking just right every minute.

It's important to understand that not only are your parents separate from you, but that they are also at a different point of life than you are. They are not as self-conscious and are likely to be more confident of their own feelings and opinions. So they're more likely to wear what they enjoy or say what they think or ask questions (like at school open houses) that you wouldn't *dream* of asking.

Keep in mind that this behavior affects you most because you still feel very tied to them—while, at the same time, you're working hard at being your own person. In the junior high years, this embarrassment happens a lot. Think about your friends—and your friends' parents. Have you noticed that most of these parents aren't nearly as embarrassing as yours? Do you find yourself thinking that some of them are almost cool? Your friends may secretly think the same thing about *your* parents. You're more tolerant of other people's parents because you're not as closely tied to them and you don't feel a particular need to prove you're separate from them.

Just remember that these are tough years not only for you, but also for your parents. They may be happy to see you growing up, but sad to see you growing away—as you *must* to become an independent person. You're going to have your differences. You're going to be exasperated with each other at times. You may end up embarrassing *each other* in different ways, for different reasons.

What may help, in between all the embarrassment and exasperation, is remembering that your connection is one of love. Sometimes you'll be able to influence one another's habits or behavior with tact and love. And sometimes you'll need to tolerate each other's traits out of love and respect. In both cases, you'll make progress toward being independent and being the person you want to grow up to be!

MY PARENTS FAVOR MY SIBLING

My dad used to be my best friend. We did lots of things together. But now he acts like he doesn't know me. He favors my little sister and takes her all the places he used to take me. I hate her and feel like beating up on her and then running away just to show him!

Jill O.

What do you do when everyone compares you unfavorably to younger brothers and sisters? My parents go on and on about how cute my three-year-old sister is and what a perfect person my ten-year-old brother is and I'm just a problem. They pick on me and say I'm too moody and my skin is bad. What can I do—besides leaving home?

Nate G.

If your parents suddenly seem to be treating you differently, ask yourself:

• Am I acting different around *them*? (For example, am I quieter? Do I choose to spend more time in my room? Do I decline to do some of the things I used to do with them?)

It could be that your parents are taking cues from you and trying to respect your new need for privacy. Or maybe they're uneasy because they don't quite know how you want to be treated. Or maybe they see you growing up and think you don't need them as much—so they turn their attention to younger children.

Keep in touch by volunteering information you feel comfortable sharing with them. Express your need for time together and suggest some activities. If you want to do something with a parent that you used to do as a child, say so. Your parent might not realize how much this would mean to you. Let your parents know when you need them. They're not mind readers.

• Have they always preferred kids of a certain age?

Some people are most at ease with babies or small children. Some people prefer teenagers. If your parents are used to dealing with younger kids and you're the first teenager in the family, they might not quite know what to do with you. Their insecurity may cause them to focus on the younger kids more because they feel better able to deal with them.

You may be able to reach out to a parent by expressing your feelings about the situation: "I feel hurt and alone because we don't seem as close as we used to. I feel left out." This is much better than taking revenge on a seemingly favored younger sibling, and may help your parents realize that you still need them—and that it may be well worth their time to *learn* how to deal with a kid who isn't really a kid anymore.

If your parents don't respond to this, if they can't cope with someone who isn't totally dependent on them, realize that this is a problem that they have and has nothing to do with your value as a person and your loveability. Seek out another adult relative—a grandparent, a special aunt or uncle, an older cousin, a family friend or neighbor or special teacher—who can fill the gap a bit and help you in ways that your parents aren't able to at the moment.

- Does one of your siblings have a special problem right now that requires your parents' attention?

Parents have a tendency to give a special helping of love and attention to the child who needs them most at any particular time. If you have a brother or sister who is chronically ill or handicapped, it may seem that your parents *always* favor them and expect too much of you. Or maybe you have a sibling who is having a lot of problems at school or a drinking or drug problem, and it seems all your parents think about or talk about is this kid. You may feel tempted, at times, to get into trouble yourself just so your parents will notice (because they sure don't seem to be taking note of the fact that you're going along doing everything right).

Resist this temptation. It's true that parents often give more attention to negative behavior than positive traits. When you're cleaning your room, going to school, doing fine, they may react with, "Well, of course. That's what you *should* be doing!" Parents need to give their teens more credit for doing the expected and beyond. So what can you do about this?

It helps to talk in a way that doesn't sound whiney or like you're accusing them of not caring. You might say something like, "I know you've been worried about Mark and I understand that he needs you a lot right now. But I need you, too. Can we spend some time together so I can tell you what's going on with me? Maybe we could take a walk together or I could help you with grocery shopping and talk to you then. It's really important for me to spend some time alone with you and to tell you about the good things—and not so good things—that are happening to me right now."

- Do your parents have a cultural or traditional reason to treat one of your siblings in a more favorable way?

This can be really tough—and especially painful because you may feel power-less to do anything about this.

Maybe in your family—because of your ethnic background or simply because your family is super-traditional—sons are prized and treated like royalty (not being expected to do any chores around the house, getting more attention and less criticism). And you, alas, are a daughter—and feel like a semi-invisible drudge, doing all the household chores while the prince of the house gets all the privileges.

Or maybe you're a boy in a home where daughters are protected and not expected to work while in school, but your parents are already insisting that you learn to make your way in the world by getting up at an unspeakably early hour to ride your bike through snow, sleet, hail, and other tortures of nature, delivering newspapers or spending half your life and every moment of your free time bagging groceries.

If parents are somehow programmed to pamper a son (or a daughter) while expecting a lot of a daughter (or a son), there may not be much you can do to change their way of thinking. But you *can* change your view of the matter. Your parents may not love you less, but are simply seeing you and your sibling in very different, sex-determined roles. This way of thinking can be much more limiting, actually, to the sibling who seems favored. If a boy doesn't learn to wash his own clothes, cook, and clean, he'll be at a real disadvantage when he's on his own (most people don't marry right out of school these days), and at a greater disadvantage in marriage when it's quite likely his wife will work outside the home out of necessity and be less than charmed at the idea of washing his socks and picking up after him just because he hasn't learned to become a self-sufficient, grown-up person.

In the same way, a girl who has been over-protected may find it difficult to cope when she doesn't have her parents there to meet her needs and solve her problems. If she's like most, she, too, will be on her own for a time before marrying and she will probably spend a good portion of her life working outside the home. Lack of experience in dealing with the real world of work and solving problems on her own can be a real disadvantage.

So if you seem unfavored right now, your parents may be doing you a favor, whether they know it or not! Learning survival skills and responsibility early on can make you a more competent person later on.

Many parents tend to be somewhat more protective of daughters than sons, insisting on strict curfews for the daughter and more or less letting the son roam free. This protectiveness is based on parents' fears—and they fear that more bad things can happen to a girl at this time of life than to a boy. That may or may not be true.

How can you deal with this? Probably the *best* way to cope is to be as responsible as possible—always being in when expected, letting your parents know (truthfully) where you're going and with whom. This way, by going along with the rules, you show your parents you're mature, responsible, and can be trusted. *Then,* in a calm, reasonable way, talk with them about easing the restrictions a bit. They may be more likely to agree when you have been responsible and when you approach them in a mature way.

Keep in mind, too, that some differences in the way parents treat you and a sibling may be more age-related than sex-related. Older siblings, ideally, have more privileges *and* more responsibilities. You will have these, too, when you're their age. In the same way, if you have more to do around the house than a younger brother or sister, it may be because you're *able* to do more—and because your parents are preparing you for true independence. Your younger siblings' time will come. They may end up having even more work around the house than you do if they reach their teens when you're off to college or working and have your own apartment—and they're left at home to do all the chores you used to share.

- Do your parents seem to favor a sibling who shares a special interest with them or who more closely meets their own particular values?

Parents are people, too, and it's a real temptation to spend a lot of time with a child who shares a special interest with them or to give special applause to a child who accomplishes something they always wanted to accomplish. So if you're an artistic type in a family of accountants (and you have a sibling who was practically born with a calculator in his hand), you may feel misunderstood and unappreciated at times. Or if you have a sibling who is a top student or unbelievably beautiful or very conspicuously talented in some way—and that seems to be all your parents care about or can talk about—you may feel alone and forgotten.

Sometimes you can help your parents—and yourself—by teaching them more about your special interest or talent so they can better appreciate your unique skills. It can help sometimes to tell your parents how you're feeling without running down your sibling or criticizing your parents. Just tell them that you feel left out, that you need their love and approval, too, even though you're quite different from your brother or sister.

There may be times when nothing much helps, and you need to give yourself credit for being your own unique person, live through the hurt, and reach out to others—friends your age and other adults—who *will* appreciate the special person you are.

MY PARENTS WON'T LET ME HAVE ANY PRIVACY

What do you do about a mother who reads your letters and your diary? Nothing is private around here! She snoops around my room when I'm at school. This makes me mad! How can I get her to stop?

Jennifer K.

I have an embarrassing problem: my mother barges in my room whenever she feels like it, even when I'm getting dressed. In her eyes, I'm five years old, but I'm really 13 and I like my privacy. How can I tell her?

Adam C.

What can I do about a little brat of a brother who comes in the bathroom whenever I'm in there just to be a brat? I'm 12 and I don't like people—any people—to see me undressed, especially this little monster (he's six) who teases me about my body and stuff. We're not allowed to lock the bathroom door around here. I'm really worried that when I get my period, he'll come in and see and I'd just die! What can I do about this?

Kim Y.

My mom wants to know everything that happens at school every day. I used to tell her everything, but now it bugs me. I don't have anything to hide, but I just don't feel like telling her everything. What's the matter with me?

Casey T.

Casey, Kim, Adam, and Jennifer are all growing up—and needing more privacy.

Having private thoughts, experiences and moments of privacy is all part of becoming your own person.

Feeling the need for privacy when dressing or when in the bathroom is also a normal part of growing up—and quite understandable as your body changes.

But some people have a tough time getting any privacy. And some people need more than others. You may feel happier on your own and need more time alone than other people in your family—and that can be hard for them to understand.

Or maybe you live in a fairly crowded house or apartment where it's almost impossible to be alone. Certainly, someone who is sharing a bedroom with one or more siblings isn't going to have as much privacy as someone with his or her own room. And if you're sleeping on the living room couch or some other makeshift arrangement, you'll have even *less* space to call your own.

And some parents have a tough time understanding your need for privacy. Out of love or concern or fear or their own unwillingness to see you growing up, they want to know everything and seek this information not only with constant questions, but also by snooping through your room. Or a parent may make a habit of reading your diary or mail because he or she doesn't really see you as a separate person yet.

Sometimes parents snoop because they feel they're losing touch with you or because they fear you're headed for or are in trouble. So they invade your privacy with all the best, most loving intentions.

What can you do?

To start, realize that your desire for some privacy is a normal part of growing up. Part of your growing independence may be to keep some things to yourself. These may be little things, as Casey points out, but they're *yours* and you may not feel like sharing all of these with parents or even with friends. Or you want to share these in your own way and when you choose (not necessarily when they ask).

Choosing what you will share and what you will keep to yourself is part of becoming your own person. It's not easy to express this need without sounding rude or disrespectful or like you have something horrible to hide. And sometimes the more you fuss about wanting privacy, the more suspicious and snoopy your parents become.

Before talking with your parents, ask yourself if you might be shutting them out of your life more than necessary—and that may be why they're so desperate to find out what you're up to. Do you answer their questions with grunts and growls? Do you spend all your time at home holed up in your room, eating meals there when you can get away with it? Do you adamantly refuse to be seen with your parents in public? If this sounds familiar at all, your parents may simply be feeling left out of your life. You *can* have privacy and you *can* be your own person without exiling your parents.

Talk with them. Tell them how much you love and appreciate them. Explain that you need some privacy now that you're older. It's reasonable to expect people to knock before coming into your room and to respect your privacy when dressing or when you're in the bathroom. Tell your parents that you're more self-conscious about your body now and get embarrassed when family members barge in on you. Ask them (calmly) for their help if younger brothers or sisters are violating your privacy just to tease. And if parents say, "Oh, for heaven's sake! I used to change your diapers and give you baths. You don't have to be embarrassed around me!" you might smile and say, "That's true, you did. But I'm not a baby anymore. Maybe I'm especially self-conscious right now because my body is changing. But I know that, for now, I do need more privacy."

If your parents have been reading diaries or letters, or listening in on telephone conversations, ask them if there's something they're especially concerned about. You may get some clues about how you can reassure them. Explain that, in growing up to be your own person, you need little bits of privacy—and that keeping your diary or letters or phone conversations private is important to you, not because you're trying to hide something. It's just important to have something separate that's all your own. Reassure them that you do love and respect them and will tell them if you have a problem or ask for help or advice when you need it. Tell them that you're not trying to hide anything major from them, but trying to be a little more independent.

It may be helpful, too, to make an effort to respect your parents' privacy. Do you interrupt their phone conversations or barge into their room or hang around when their friends visit, or borrow things without asking or read their private mail? Decide together the boundaries for privacy in your home and then respect them. If your parents know you respect their privacy, they may be more likely to respect yours.

You might try to find ways to compromise. Maybe it would be all right to lock the bathroom door *if* you don't stay in there so long that you inconvenience others. Maybe your parents would feel fine about your taking the phone into your room to talk privately *if* you observe a certain time limit. Maybe they'll leave your diary alone or stop bugging you about every detail of your day *if* you give them more information than a testy grunt at the dinner table.

But sometimes this doesn't work. There are some parents who don't think that kids of any age—and that includes teens—should have any privacy. They feel they have an absolute right to know everything, however minor. Or they may feel very upset whenever you assert your individuality or independence. This is a problem for them that they may be able to resolve only over time.

In the meantime, you might get a few moments of privacy by taking a long walk when you need to be alone. Or volunteer to run errands or to do yardwork by yourself to get some time alone. Remember that you can have a very separate and private life of your own—in your mind! You can do a lot of growing to be your own unique person in that quiet way. You can nurture your own independence by enjoying your own thoughts, plans, and dreams for the future.

MY PARENTS DON'T CARE ABOUT ME ANYMORE

I'm 13 and upset. My dad used to hug me a lot and spend lots of time with me. Now he acts like a stranger. What did I do to make him hate me?

Petra G.

Some of my friends complain about their parents being around and on their case all the time. I have the opposite problem. As soon as I started junior high last year, my mom went back to work and now she doesn't get home until 6 or 7, if she doesn't have a meeting or something. My dad is starting his own business which takes a lot of his time and he's worried about money a lot. So when he's home, he's a grouch. I don't have any brothers or sisters and it gets kind of lonely around here. My parents say they have to work these long hours, but they never did before last year. Sometimes I think they don't care about me anymore.

Brent L.

What can you do about a dad who's a health nut? I used to like sitting around with my dad on weekends watching sports on TV. Now, since he turned 40, he's going crazy and thinks he's a big athlete or something! He's always out running or meeting some friend or the other to play tennis or squash and he's talking about taking golf lessons, too. I wish I had my old dad back.

Jeff N.

Just when you're facing so many changes, your parents may be changing, too. Some of these changes may be in their relationship with you.

For example, some dads act like Petra's father, withdrawing from daughters and not showing as much affection. If this is happening to you, it may help to know that this probably has very little to do with your dad's love for you. Some fathers simply need time to adjust to the fact that you're not a little girl anymore. When your body starts changing to that of a young woman, your father may feel a little uncomfortable with you and not know quite how to treat you as an emerging young woman. This doesn't mean that his love for you is less. It just means that he needs time, too, to adjust to your changes. If he doesn't hug you as much or wrestle like he used to, it could be that he doesn't want to offend you in any way. If you need a hug, ask him. You might say, "I know I'm growing up pretty fast. But I still need hugs and your love just as I always have."

Sometimes your parents' lives are changing because they feel you're old enough to look after yourself a lot of the time and so are taking a bit of the focus off you and putting it onto their own deferred goals and dreams. It's understandable . . . but can be a shock when you still find yourself needing your parents a lot.

What can you do?

First, you need to accept the fact that times are changing for all of you. Your parents may be entering the most demanding phases of their careers. As they see you growing up and away from them, spending more and more time with friends, they may be rediscovering each other. Also, your parents may be facing various crises of middle age—re-evaluating their lives and their priorities—and don't have as much energy to focus on you right now.

Second, you must communicate your needs to them. When you really need to talk with or be with your parents, let them know. For example, tell your parents that you need an evening to spend together as a family or need time to talk alone with one of them every day, or whatever it is you need. Then, together, decide how this might be arranged. If your parents are like most, they'll do everything they can to be there for you.

On the other hand, you need to be realistic. Maybe they can't be there for you as much as they used to be or in quite the same way. You may need to do some compromising, too.

For example:

- If your parent has ceased to be a couch potato and is a budding middle-aged athlete, suggest that you exercise together at least some of the time. Taking a walk together can be a great time for a private talk. Running or working out at the gym together can bring you closer in a new way.
- If one or both parents tends to be grouchy right after getting home from work, don't hit them with your needs right away. Give them half an hour or an hour to relax. Ask when you might have a talk. Or regularly set some time aside to talk, to ask for homework help, or whatever you need.
- If you wish your parents had more free time for you, help them to get more free time. If you have dinner started before they get home from work and get together to clean up the kitchen afterwards or do some household chores they usually do after work, or if you go with them to do things like grocery shopping, this will give your parents more free time to spend with you. Working together can also give you time to share the events of the day.
- Be flexible. Maybe, in the past, you fell into the pattern a lot of people do: you would keep a parent in suspense about your day, your feelings, or other things important to you or to them until you felt like sharing these. Maybe this would be several hours after they asked. When time is at a premium, this suspense-building tactic may be a luxury you can't afford. You may need to talk with your parents at times they're available to you. They may not have the time or patience these days to hang around waiting. So if there's something you really need to talk over, give yourself the benefit of their full attention—whenever that happens to be available.

It's important to remember that, as busy or preoccupied as they might be, your parents still love you and care very much about you. By thoughtfulness on both sides and some careful planning, you can still spend time together and be important to each other. You can help this along by letting your parents know what you feel and what you need—and by being sensitive to their changing lives as well.

MY PARENTS EXPECT TOO MUCH

My parents expect me to be perfect. Really! My mother is always fussing at me about my clothes and looking my best and being popular. My dad wants me to make all "A's" and thinks I ought to go to medical school after college. I get really grossed out when I'm around someone sick, so I can't see myself doing that. The thing is, I'm only 13 and I feel they've got my whole life planned, but it doesn't have anything to do with what I want. I'm really upset about this.

Rachel R.

I'm a "B" student and have to work very hard for my grades. But my parents are convinced I'm a genius and every time I get a report card, I get punished for not doing better. They won't listen when I say I'm doing the best I can. Now I'm grounded for the entire year with no phone, radio, or TV privileges. What's the point of working so hard if I just get punished for it?

"Thirteen and Miserable"

My parents expect me to be more grown up than I am and don't let me have any life of my own. I can't do any after school activities because I have to be home to take care of my younger brother and start supper. On weekends, they expect me to baby-sit him (for no money, naturally!). I never get to go out or to take baby-sitting jobs that would pay money. And if I forget to do something, even something small like curling up the hose on the patio after watering all the plants, they carry on like I'd committed a terrible crime. I'm 12, but I feel like I'm 80 and in jail! What can I do?

Monica P.

As you grow up, your parents' expectations of you grow as well. They expect you to act more adult, to take on more family responsibilities, to do the best you can do. Ideally, parents want the best for you in all ways and give you loving encouragement to achieve your goals and dreams.

But sometimes there is a problem.

Maybe your parents, like Monica's, expect you to take on too many responsibilities too soon.

Maybe your parents expect you to be a sports superstar or a top student without taking your real abilities, desires, and feelings into account.

Maybe your parents keep changing the rules so that when you meet one expectation and start to feel proud of yourself, you're still falling short of what they expect.

Maybe your parents expect you to fulfill their own long-lost dreams: to be a doctor or an actress or, more immediately, extremely popular in school or a cheerleader.

Whatever impossible expectations you might be facing, it's important to remember that your value as a person is not linked to your grades, whether or not you win prizes, make the cheerleading squad, get into a prestigious college or anything else. You are a worthwhile person with or without these things.

If your parents' expectations are unrealistically high, there may be several reasons why.

If they expect you to do more than you feel able around the house or in taking care of siblings, maybe they are especially overburdened right now. Or maybe they don't realize how this is affecting you. It could be, if you mention your need to have more time with your friends, or to pursue certain activities, in a calm way without accusing them of taking advantage of you, they will try to arrange things so that you do have more free time. If you're willing to work with them and to compromise, too, you may be able to work out an arrangement everybody feels is fair.

If your parents are very critical of things you do around the house, tell them that you're trying your best. You're not going to be a gourmet cook all at once. If you suddenly find yourself with many more chores, you're not always going to remember them all or do them perfectly at first. Sometimes parents forget what it's like to have all these new responsibilities or to learn a new skill. If you're having trouble with one or two tasks in particular, ask for help. Let them know that you're willing to learn, but that it may take a little time to do it just right.

If your parents have really impossible expectations for you, this may come from their own dissatisfaction with themselves. If they're not happy with themselves, they may never be completely pleased by anyone else, including you. As hard as you try, their expectations will always be a step ahead of your achievements.

What can you do?

Start TODAY to set your own goals and to do your best for *you*. If you know that you're trying your best and that you're working toward goals that are all your own, your parents' unrealistic expectations might not hurt quite as much. You might even feel a little sorry for your perfectionist parent. Just think of all the joy they're missing when they can't enjoy you as you are—or themselves as they are.

If you're being punished despite your best efforts, try talking with an adult who may be able to help you. This person might be able to help you feel good about yourself and/or may be able to talk with your parents. This caring adult might be a favorite teacher or school counselor or another relative or someone from your church or synagogue.

If, like Rachel, you feel that your life plan is being set and that it has no relation to what you want, remember that you can listen to your parents and respect their opinions, but that, when the time comes to make important life choices, you need to choose what is right for *you* and do the best you can—for *you*.

You may find, in time, that some of your parents' dreams weren't so unrealistic after all.

Maybe, after a few months, you will find that you can handle household tasks better and faster than you ever imagined.

Maybe, in years to come, a parent's career suggestion will make more sense than it does right now. That doesn't always happen. But it can.

My father used to drive me *crazy* when I was 13 with his plans for me to become a writer—and write books. I kept saying, "No way! It would be like having a term paper due all the time. I'd hate it! Forget it!" I set my sights on being . . . a ballerina or actress or even a nun . . . ANYTHING but a writer! Later, in high school and college, I slowly began to realize that writing really was what I did best. I remember thinking (a little angrily), "Oh, no, my father might have been right!" And he was, though he never said, "I told you so." But his impossible dream for me became, in time, my *own* dream for my *own* reasons and has turned into just the right career—for me. So you never know.

Of course, quite often, it doesn't turn out that way. You may have to risk disappointing your parents to do what you need and want to do. If that time comes for you, just remember that these high expectations can come from their own pain and disappointment in themselves and out of their love and hope for you.

Most parents want, above all, for their children to be happy. When you're happy and doing your best at what you really want in your life, your parents may well come to realize that and, in time, rejoice with you.

MY PARENTS ARE IN TROUBLE

I feel really sad and scared. My parents fight with each other all the time and then don't speak for days. I think my dad has a girlfriend, but I'm not sure. Sometimes I hate both of them and sometimes I cry because I don't want them to split up. I'm scared of what might happen.

Mandy Y.

My dad lost his job three weeks ago and it's AWFUL! He's very depressed and sleeps a lot. Mom cries a lot. He keeps saying we might have to move to a cheaper place and I'm scared of losing my friends and I get mad at him, even though I know it isn't really his fault. What can I do?

J.D.

My parents are getting a divorce and they both try to pump me for information about the other. It makes me upset. It seems like nothing will ever be fun or anything around our house ever again.

Patti K.

My mother drinks—a lot! It's so bad I'm too embarrassed to have my friends over because I don't know how she'll be. I can't ever talk to her. The house is a mess. My dad travels a lot for his job and is almost never home. Once I yelled at my mother and called her an "alcoholic," but she says she's not. It's really confusing and lonely.

Aileen R.

Living with parents in crisis can be scary, lonely, and confusing—whatever the crisis. You want to make things better for everyone, but you don't know how. You may wonder if you have contributed to your parent's drinking problem or your parents' marital woes. You might spend a lot of time wondering what's going to happen to you if . . . your parents divorce or your alcoholic parent doesn't stop drinking or a parental job loss threatens to bring some major lifestyle changes for your family.

What can you *do* when your parents have such major problems it feels like your whole world is falling apart?

Realize—Once and for All—That It's Not Your Fault. Many of us are quick to take the blame for faults or crises of those closest to us. Why? It's a way to avoid facing the fact that, when it comes to another person's crisis, we're powerless to change it or to keep life exactly the same.

Even if your parents *say* you've driven them to drink or to divorce, it probably isn't so. A strong, loving marriage can survive many family storms and stresses. Even if parental arguments have centered on you primarily, your parents are fighting and perhaps breaking up for their own reasons—including anger at each other that may only get expressed through you. An alcoholic parent may drink for a multitude of reasons, including a possible inherited tendency to drink to excess.

When you realize that your parents' crisis is NOT your fault, it does take away the idea that you can magically do anything to solve the problem. But this realization can also FREE you to rise above these problems and find your own way of dealing with them.

Don't Allow Yourself to Be Drawn Into the Middle of the Problem. A parent who is very troubled or unhappy may, in his or her own efforts to deny the problem, try to blame another or convince another person to take responsibility for solving everything. The best way to deal with this is to refuse to play the game.

For example, if your parents fight a lot or if they're divorced and don't speak to each other most of the time, they may try to use you as a messenger between them or may try to get you to take one side or the other. Either way, you lose.

Instead, say, "I love you both and I don't want to keep you from working out your problems in your own way." Or you might say, "I love you both and that's why I really don't feel comfortable acting as a spy or messenger. I would like the freedom to spend time with and love you both."

When they try to get you involved in their fights, your parents probably aren't trying to hurt you. *They're* hurting a lot and just not thinking. It may be up to *you* to tell them how you feel about what they're asking of you and why you need to say "No."

Whenever Possible, Ease Your Demands on a Troubled Parent. If your parents are going through a scary, troubled time, like money problems, this is *not* the time to ask for nonessentials. This may be the time to suggest a very simple Christmas with lots of carols and togetherness and few, if any, presents. This may be a time to make do with older school clothes instead of expecting a whole new wardrobe. This may be the time to look into a paper route or baby-sitting jobs to earn some of your own pocket money.

In the same way, if your parents are going through a painful time, like a divorce, they may not be there for you emotionally the way they used to be. This is a time to save your arguments only for *really* important things instead of getting into it with them over every little thing. This is a time to do chores without being nagged. This may also be the time to talk over some of your own problems with other adults who have the time and energy to listen: older relatives, a neighbor, a teacher. That way, you can get some of the attention you need even though your parents are temporarily unable to give it.

If you have a parent with a serious addiction problem, and if you are trying to rescue him or her by screaming, yelling, and throwing the alcohol or drugs down the drain, you may be adding to rather than solving the problem. It's likely that your parent will go right on drinking. And the parent will focus his or her anger on you and thus find yet another excuse not to deal with his or her own problem. Some people with serious drinking problems have no motivation to change until things get very, very bad for them.

Realize That You Will Have a Lot of Different Feelings About Your Situation—and All of These Are Normal. Your feelings about your family or your troubled parent or parents are probably very complicated. Sometimes you feel very loving and want, more than anything, to help. Sometimes you feel so angry you can hardly stand it. You might feel like screaming, crying, or yelling at the person. You may feel like running away or feel so hopeless that you can't imagine things getting better—and you become furious at your parents, even if the problem is something one or both couldn't help. For example, maybe your mom or dad lost a job through no fault of his or her own—and it means you have to move. That really makes you mad because you'll be leaving your friends. It's normal to feel mad about this. You're possibly losing some friends that are very important to you right now. (You might feel better if you can keep in touch by letters or phone and occasional visits with these friends so you won't really lose them totally.) Maybe you feel guilty because you're mad about something a parent can't help. Maybe your dad left your mom— which really broke her heart—and you find yourself taking out all your anger on *her.* And that seems crazy. But it isn't. If you are living with a parent whose love is not in doubt, you may feel safe and comfortable enough to express angry feelings. With a parent you're not as close to, you may not feel confident enough in their love to let them know how you really feel.

Of course, these feelings don't need to be expressed in a hurtful way. It may help to write your feelings in a diary or talk to some friends whose parents are also divorced, or who have lost a parent by death, or who have a family situation somewhat like yours. It may help to talk with a grandparent or an older brother or sister. Or hug and talk to a pet. (This can help you to relax and to hear some of your own feelings expressed out loud.)

Seek Support From People Who Really Understand. Do you have a parent who drinks too much? It can be scary and embarrassing, especially if your friends notice that your parent has a problem. It can help a lot to go to Ala-Teen meetings. (You can find out about these by looking in the white pages of your phone book under "Ala-Teen" or "Al-Anon.") These organizations are related to Alcoholics Anonymous and are for children and families of alcoholics. These groups can help you find ways to separate yourself from your parent's problem and to cope with your feelings by sharing them with people who really understand—young people like you who have one or more alcoholic parents. In this group, you can learn to act in ways that *don't* encourage your parent's drinking. You'll learn how to stop trying to rescue your troubled parent, let go with love, and live your own life.

If your parents fight a lot or are divorced, you can find special support, too. Some school systems and communities have support groups for children of single parents. And many, many more young people these days are growing up in families divided by divorce. It isn't at all unusual. That doesn't mean that it's not terribly painful. But, if you look around, you will notice there are a lot of classmates who have faced many of the same problems. You're not alone.

I HAVE TOO MANY PARENTS!

My mother's boyfriend thinks he can tell me what to do. If my mom asks me to do something, I'll do it. It's the same with my dad when I'm with him. But when Joe, her boyfriend, starts trying to act like he's my father and orders me around, I don't want to do anything he says. This gets me in trouble with my mom. What should I do?

Brandon K.

I'm upset. My dad recently married a woman with two really bratty little boys, ages seven and nine. I'm 12. I hate her because she bosses me around and doesn't let me be alone with my dad ever! Also, my dad is super nice to her kids and never punishes them, even when they deserve it. I think he likes them more than me!

Kate O.

I'm 11 and confused. My parents are divorced and both of them have married other people. When I spend time with my dad and his wife, I have one set of rules. When I spend time with Mom and her husband (I live with them most of the time), I have another set of rules. It's confusing. What should I do?

Sherri-Lynn A.

Life can get pretty complicated when you have so many people, some of them new, acting like parents. It can be confusing, especially if all these people have different rules. It can be irritating, particularly if a new person is acting like a parent and telling you what to do right away. And when a parent remarries and suddenly there are other kids in the family—new babies or stepbrothers or stepsisters, it's easy to feel jealous, scared of losing your parent's love and attention, left out and forgotten.

What can you do?

If, like Brandon, one (or both) of your parents has a new love who tries to be a parent to you right away and upsets you with orders and even punishment, it may be tempting to fight back with that person or to try to cause trouble between your parent and the new love so your parent will drop that person and things can get back to normal around your house.

But all that can be pretty uncomfortable for everyone, including you, and it doesn't always work. You may end up with your parent mad at you and resenting the fact that you're trying to make trouble. He or she may even insist that you obey the new love, which only makes things worse.

A better tactic: Sometime when you're alone, tell your mom or dad how you feel. You might say something like, "I don't want to cause trouble between you and ____, but I really feel angry when he(she) comes in here without knowing me well and starts telling me what to do or punishing me. I feel that's your role. I will do whatever you want or ask me to do. I will respect your friend as I would respect any adult. But I would prefer to get orders, directions, and punishment from you. Maybe my feelings will change when I know ____ better. But for now, I really need just one parent here—and that's you."

This is a reasonable request and, if you present it to your parent in a calm, respectful way, he or she may listen and ask his/her friend to back off. Many times, adults who are dating people with children don't know quite how to act or what is expected of them, so they start acting like another parent—not to be mean—but because they don't know any better. And some parents, new to dating, aren't used to having another adult around and might just fall into letting that person act like a parent. If it bothers you, letting your parent know in a respectful way can help.

It can also help to decide what matters and what doesn't. If your parent's new love asks you to do something that doesn't matter to you one way or the other or something that you would probably do anyway, it may not be worth digging in your heels and refusing just because this person asked you to do it. You won't be losing and he/she won't be winning. Life will simply be easier for all of you if you just go ahead and do whatever it is. Save your battles for the things that are really important to you.

Living by two very different sets of rules at Mom's house and Dad's house *can* be confusing.

Resist the temptation to say to the parent who is stricter, "But *Dad (Mom)* lets me . . ." That is guaranteed to make your parent even more convinced that you should—and will—follow his or her own rules exactly.

If the rule conflict is really upsetting to you and is creating big problems in your life, ask—again respectfully—that your parents get together on their own and work out some sort of agreement.

But if it's just sort of confusing and irritating or if your parents can't agree on *anything,* you may have to settle for living with two sets of rules, respecting the rules of the house wherever you happen to be. You can get used to this . . . and it may even help you to grow in your ability to get along with a variety of people with different viewpoints.

Think of it in positive terms: Some kids have to live with one set of parents who may be as strict as your strictest set of parents. At least you have a choice to spend some time with parents who may not be quite as strict. You don't have to live constantly with just one set of rules!

If you resent a new stepparent, that's not so unusual. After all, this person is getting a big portion of your parent's love, and sometimes you may wonder if there's enough love left for you. Or you may have been hoping that your parents would get back together and then along comes this new person and spoils everything!

It isn't that simple, of course. People divorce for a lot of reasons and, even if one of your parents did happen to be involved with another person before the divorce, this person did not *cause* the divorce. Happily married people who love each other do not allow an outsider to come between them. Chances are, your parents' marriage was in trouble well before that other person came along. And, once they part, most people *don't* come back together again, no matter how much they love their children and want the best for them. Deciding to split up a family is a very painful decision—and one that is rarely made on a whim.

Many of us who grew up reading fairy tales about wicked stepparents may be convinced that they come in only one variety: cruel and uncaring. But that isn't so. Few stepmothers (or fathers) are truly wicked. And few of them, on the other hand, are perfect parents—especially at first, when they're trying to adjust to a new marriage *and* a new, instant family. They're dealing with some big changes, too, which is why they may make lots of mistakes at first. It will take time for all of you to get used to one another. You may end up being close—or you may not. But you *can* learn to tolerate each other.

It can be especially tough when you're dealing with a changing family—not just a new stepmother or stepfather, but stepsiblings or a new baby half brother or half sister. Again, you may wonder if there's enough love and attention to go around and you may wonder why your parent seems to be so much easier on his or her stepchildren than on you.

Usually, this is not due to lack of love for you, but the fact that your parent is comfortable with you, secure in your love for each other, and feels very much like your parent. With new stepchildren, on the other hand, he or she may still be getting to know them and may have an agreement that he/she will let the new spouse, who is the parent to those kids, do the disciplining—at least for a while.

It may be likely, too, that when your parents are busy adjusting to a new family, there may not be as much time for everyone to get the same amount of attention for a while.

Dr. Alayne Yates is a psychiatrist who had seven children of her own when she married a man with six children. She says that it took about two to three years for everyone to adjust and accept one another.

What can you do in the meantime if you're feeling left out?

"Look to grandparents, other relatives, and friends to fill the gap for you during this transition time," Dr. Yates suggests. "It can also help to have regular family conferences to air feelings and figure out how to solve problems. That's a lot better than arguing among each other all the time and taking sides or feeling quietly angry and jealous because all these people are sharing your parent's love and attention. Talking about feelings and needs and setting up some rules together can help a lot."

MY PARENTS CAN'T COMMUNICATE WITH ME!

I'm always fighting with my mom. My parents are divorced and I never see my dad, who lives 500 miles away. Either I mouth off to my mom or she screams at me about the smallest thing. We can't talk to each other without fighting! I can hardly wait to leave home, but I'm still just 14 and I can't live with my dad because he doesn't want me to. It's like World War III around here. I'm not kidding!!! What can I do?

David A.

My parents don't understand me. Not at all. It's like we're from two different planets. I'd like to tell them how I feel about things, but it seems useless.

Elizabeth C.

Lack of communication can run both ways. Your parents may assume that they're always right, that your job is to listen and theirs is to talk—and that's it. Or you may have the idea that your parents are so old and out of it, they would never understand what it's like to be young in today's world. These assumptions can get in the way of communication. If you want to start communicating with your parents—and if they feel the same—here are some suggestions.

Stop Making Assumptions About Each Other! No matter how old and out of it they seem, your parents do remember what it was like to be young. If it seems they've forgotten, or the theme of most of their talks is "I don't want you to make the same mistakes *I* made!" they're very busy being concerned parents. But that doesn't mean that it would be impossible for them to understand your point of view.

In the same way, it isn't fair for parents to think that, just because you're young, you're going to make every mistake there is to make or every one they made when they were young. You're a different person. And, too often, adults assume that just because you're young, you have no idea what love really is or what it means to be really scared or disappointed or depressed. The fact is, your feelings are valid and real. When you're older, your circumstances may change. The kind of person you will love in years to come may change. But feelings know no age limit. And people of all ages need to understand that.

Instead of making assumptions, accept the fact that you and your parents are separate people, at different points in your lives, but people who feel many of the same things and who have a lot to share with each other.

Respect Each Other As People. You can respect someone, even when you disagree with him or her. That person is entitled to his or her point of view and you're entitled to yours. Agreement isn't always the ultimate sign of love. You can strongly disagree—and still love and respect each other very much.

It's also important now that you're older, to see each other in a new way: as imperfect people who love each other. When you were little, you probably thought your parents were perfect. Now you know they're not. Now that you're older and wiser, you know—deep down—that it's not reasonable to expect your parents to be patient all the time, to never make mistakes. Sometimes they'll be patient and sometimes they'll be short-tempered. Sometimes they'll be very wise and sometimes they'll be wrong. It's very hard for some parents to admit it when they're wrong, especially when they know you see their mistake. In the same way, it can be tough for parents to accept your differences, your own shortcomings, and your own right to be wrong.

It may take you time to get used to all of this . . . but when you can respect each other as separate people and agree to disagree as gently as possible, you're on the way to better communication.

Listen to Each Other! Communication is blocked when people want to talk, but don't bother to listen to each other. This makes it easy to misunderstand each other, to have a little disagreement escalate to a major fight and make all of you feel pretty hopeless about ever communicating with each other.

First, try listening to your parents as they talk about their feelings and values instead of breaking in to argue or shutting them out while you plan what to say. Listen quietly and with respect. Then, when they are finished, tell them in a calm way what your feelings are. If you have listened to your parents, they're MUCH more likely to listen to you.

Second, if you are listening to your parents, but they aren't giving you equal time, try talking with them during a relaxed moment. Tell your parents that you respect their feelings and opinions, whether or not you agree with them, and that it's really important to you that they also listen to how you feel. You might present this as a possible solution, saying, "If you know how I feel, too, then maybe we'll be able to understand each other better and find ways to decide on rules without arguing so much."

Accept the Fact That You Can Love Each Other—and Still Disagree. You can disagree intensely and still love each other. Sometimes this means keeping an opinion to yourself or airing it only with friends because you know you and your parents will never agree. That can save a lot of needless fighting.

But often this means disagreeing in a gentle way: "I understand what you're saying and I respect your feelings. I feel differently, but I don't expect you to change your mind just to please me."

Often, it's enough to leave it at that. However, if your disagreement is about a rule or plan of action, you might add, "Let's think—together—of a way we can work this out so we can all feel good about it."

Things won't always work out so well, of course. There will be arguments. There may be times when you cry and rage together. There may be times when you feel impossibly far apart. You may grow to realize that you and your parents will always have very different views and, perhaps, very different lives.

That doesn't mean that you can't be close to each other, important to each other, or love each other very much. When you want and work toward better communication, you may find that, in spite of all your differences, you will always have many thoughts and feelings and much love to share with each other.

CHAPTER THREE

The Changing School Scene

I'm scared about starting junior high in September. Where I am now, we're the class everyone looks up to. But next year, we'll be the babies again. I hate the thought of being teased and looked down on and bossed around. I asked my parents if I could go to this private school that two of my friends will be going to that goes up to eighth grade, but my parents said that we can't afford it and, besides, starting a new school would be just about like starting my new junior high. Some people I know are looking forward to it, but I'm scared!

Erin R.

I've been in seventh grade for a week and I hate it!! I can't get my locker open half the time, I've been late to all my classes because of this, people steal my lunch, everyone hates me, and the teachers are mean. What can I do?

P.N.

Starting a new school is hard enough. Starting junior high—at a time when you're going through so many physical and emotional changes—can be a real shock. If you're going from a K–6 elementary school to a 7–9 or 7 and 8 junior high or middle school, you're facing some big changes. The atmosphere will be less personal, with classroom and teacher changes each period, and many new faces among your classmates. There will be locker combinations to remember (this, according to recent studies, is one of the greatest concerns young people just starting junior high have), class schedules to memorize, and a faster pace all around.

People expect more of you: from teachers who start talking about doing well so you can go on to achieve in high school and college to classmates who put a new emphasis on fashion and popularity and who is "in" and who is "out." It's a time when being popular with the opposite sex takes on new importance, and a time when your body is going through so many changes that you feel self-conscious just when you need all the confidence you can get!

It *is* very difficult to go from being the top class at elementary school to the low class on the status ladder in your new school. You may be in for some teasing and bossing and other power games from the older classes.

What can you do when you're facing this big change?

Make It Easier on Yourself Those First Weeks. The locker and the frantic class schedules can be real challenges. Keep your locker combination on an index card in your pocket at all times. Write it on your hand or in your assignment notebook to be extra safe. Don't try to make it back to your locker between each class. Carry the books and papers you'll need for your first few class periods with you so that you can eliminate locker hassles and get to classes on time. Practice opening your locker during lunch or before or after school until you're confident. (You'll be amazed how easy it will become with time and practice!)

Keep a copy of your class schedule with you all the time so you'll always be able to look up your next class and room number in case you forget.

Get an assignment notebook and write down all homework assignments—overnight and long-term—so that you don't forget. (It's not easy juggling instructions from all those different teachers at first.)

Finally, don't expect everything to go wonderfully right away. You will make mistakes. You will feel uncomfortable for a while. You may feel lonely at times. That's all part of being in a new, more challenging school situation. In time, you'll feel more comfortable and confident.

Be Careful of Taking First Impressions (Or Rumors) Too Seriously. Your first impressions of junior high may be that it's impossibly large, that people are mostly stuck up and cold, and that the teachers all expect too much and some of them are actually mean. This may seem very true of your school at first and you may feel desperately unhappy.

Give yourself—and the school—time. Other people in your classes are busy feeling scared and wanting to belong, too. And the older classes are temporarily having a good time feeling older and wiser. They may tease, put you down, and boss you around. This will probably change in a very short time after you and your classmates start learning your way around the school and feeling more comfortable—and everyone settles down.

Be careful of taking advice you get from older students too seriously. They may tell you, "You have Mr. Smith for social studies? Oh, he's the worst! You'll hate him. He fails almost everyone." Or, "Take general math with Mrs. Simpson. You won't even have to study."

They may mean well—or not. But your experiences may be quite different from theirs. If you go into Mr. Smith's class already feeling scared and defeated, you won't be able to do your best—and maybe you *won't* get along with him. If you go in with an open mind, you may find that Mr. Smith isn't a terror at all. Maybe he's just allergic to people who don't work and don't care, but is delighted to work with students of *all* ability levels who honestly try to do their best. And if you approach Mrs. Simpson's class with the notion that this is going to be a cinch and never crack a book, you may be in for a rude shock at grading time—if not before.

So take classes because you want or need to take them and keep an open mind about the teacher.

Because teachers *do* expect more of you now that you're older, they may seem mean in comparison with some of the teachers you've had before. Actually, some of the most demanding teachers can be the most caring. They want you to learn to take responsibility and to do your best. Asking a lot of you is not being mean.

Of course, there will always be some teachers who have gruff or even mean personalities and these can be tough to take. In time, you'll learn how to keep from aggravating them and even get along with them reasonably well. That's good preparation for adult life—when you may find yourself working with or for some difficult people. You're not going to like all your teachers—or later, your coworkers or bosses—equally, but you can get along with most of them.

Realize That It's Normal, When You're Facing a Big Change, to Feel a Bit Overwhelmed at First. Most people, when starting a new phase of school, go in wondering if everyone else is smarter and more sophisticated, if they will ever fit in. Being scared or uncertain is part of dealing with change. This isn't meant to minimize how scared you may feel right now. Just remember that you can't overcome all your fear or uncertainty at once. Try to do one thing a day that helps you to feel a little more in charge.

For example, you might say "Hi" to people and start conversations without waiting for people to talk to you first, one person at first, others later on. You might give yourself a pat on the back the first time you get your locker combination right without looking at your index card. Or see if you can get to all your classes on time—and get all your assignments in—just for today. Pick out someone you knew at your old school and liked or someone new who seems pretty nice and get to know that person better. Suggest sitting together at lunch. Pick out the *least* scary challenge for you right now and enjoy your success with that. Then build on this success until school seems less and less overwhelming.

BUT I'M NOT "IN"

There is this "in" crowd of about six girls who decide everything, including who is an outcast and what the right clothes are. They decided I'm a "dog" because I'm not cute, and whenever I go by their table in the cafeteria they make barking sounds. It makes me want to cry and sometimes I do, which is embarrassing. One of them yelled that I'm a nerd because I wore a plaid skirt today and another said, "Nice skirt, Tina!" and then made gagging sounds. I wanted to disappear. But I couldn't. I'm so miserable, I can hardly stand to go to school—and all because of them.

Tina H.

What does it take to get in the in-crowd? I can't get accepted by them and I hate being a nobody. How can I get "in" when they don't know I'm alive?

Kimberly Y.

Nobody likes me. It's my second week at junior high and I hate it. I don't have anyone to eat lunch with. And some people make fun of my clothes because my mom made them. Everyone else has expensive brand clothes, but my family can't afford that. And if people knew we didn't have very much money, I'm afraid they'd hate me even more. What can I do to stop being so miserable?

Leigh Ann J.

The notorious "in" crowd exists in every school and has been making people's lives miserable for years and years.

In a recent magazine interview, Academy Award–winning actress Sally Field recalled being rejected by her junior high's in-group because she wasn't considered "cute," and going home heartbroken time after time when the girls humiliated her on the schoolbus. She would lie on the floor of her closet and wonder how she could ever go back to school, feeling "crushed, humiliated, and embarrassed down to my toes!"

Those feelings are familiar to a lot of us who weren't in the in-group—and you may be feeling this pain right now, too.

The first thing you need to realize is that, while some people associate the in-group with "popular," this isn't always so. Being in the in-group is more about power than popularity.

What gives these people such power? Unfortunately, it tends to be things that they are *given* rather than qualities they have earned. In-groupers often tend to be unusually pretty or handsome, from affluent or powerful families, and have athletic ability, and lots of stylish clothes.

When you're on the outside looking in and don't have these essential givens, it can be pretty depressing. You may wonder why people who seem so snobbish and mean can have such perfect lives and if life will always be this unfair.

Actually, if you could trade places with someone in the in-group for a day, you might find that life isn't exactly perfect. A lot of in-groupers are secretly insecure, wondering if they're liked for themselves or for their power positions. Some don't feel especially liked and some don't like the other people in the in-group, but don't feel the freedom to make other friends. Some may even realize, too, that their power is based on factors that could change. One can lose looks, money, and status. An injury could sideline an athletic (or cheerleading) career.

If you're not in the in-group, you may be at an advantage: You're free to make friends with anyone, and those who like you will like you for your own qualities, not for your power.

But it may be hard to feel lucky when people make fun of you, when nobody seems to want to be your friend. What can you do if you feel totally friendless and hopelessly out of it?

Don't Allow Yourself to Be a Victim. This *doesn't* fall into the same maddening category as the usual adult advice, "Just don't pay any attention to the people making fun of you." It's impossible to ignore someone who is barking or jeering across the lunchroom at you or who confronts you in front of your locker with daily taunts.

Instead, think of how you have reacted to this torment in the past. Have you cried? Have you been flustered or visibly upset? You may have been giving the bully what he or she wants: an upset reaction.

While it's tough to give no reaction and just ignore your tormenters, you might try throwing them off with an unexpected reaction. You might calmly (with just a touch of sarcasm) agree with them: "Oh, right, I'm a real dog. And I'm planning to wear a plaid blouse to match my skirt tomorrow just for you." Or, "You're right. I am a nerd. You wouldn't believe what a nerd I am." When you stay calm and simply agree, this takes a lot of power away from your tormenters. They're not getting what they want from you to fuel their cruel words and to feel truly powerful.

It can help, too, to take your attacker's personality into account. Is he or she known all over school as a bully? Does this person habitually say nasty things to people? That can take some of the sting out of his or her words. Even though you may feel embarrassed (humiliated is more like it!) when this person starts in on you in a very public place, the other people present know what this person is like. Most likely, they're *not* agreeing with him or her that you're a dog or a nerd or otherwise out of it. They're probably thinking two things: "Thank goodness *I'm* not the victim!" and "What a jerk! He (she) is so mean!"

If someone is seriously threatening you constantly—stealing your lunch or your lunch money, beating you up or making your life miserable with taunts, jeers, racial slurs, or the like, you may need to enlist the aid of the principal. While it's best, whenever possible, to work out differences between yourselves without getting teachers or administrators involved, some situations are too tough, too painful, or too dangerous for you to handle alone. Be prepared to give a clear, specific account of what has been happening with incidents and dates. Your parents may also be able to help you, either by rehearsing with you ways that you can face down a bully or by backing you if you have to seek help from school officials.

While most bullies can be handled with a calm attitude and well chosen words from you, it's good to know that adult help *is* available if your own efforts aren't enough.

Make It Easier for People to Know Who You Really Are. If you're shy or retiring or walk around with eyes downcast waiting for people to shower you with insults, you'll have a harder time than most making friends.

Just for today, go to school and act *as if* people liked you. Hold up your head and look at other people as you pass them in the hall. Smile. Say "Hello." Start one conversation. You'll feel better and people may start to notice you in a new way. This isn't a one-day miracle cure for loneliness, but it can help you get started in the right direction.

Look into school activities or community organizations where you can pursue special interests and talents—while meeting other people who have some of the same interests and will notice some of your special qualities.

Let the In-Group Have Their Power While You Search Out Real Friends. Take a good look at the in-group. Are they good friends to each other? Are they real friends to the people who hang around on the outside edges of the group—the people who aren't the superstars, but who are tolerated by others in the group as long as they dress or act a certain way? Are these in-group hangers-on being thrown out of the group periodically on someone's whim? That's a pretty tense way to live.

If you don't have the "givens" that the members of the in-group at your school have (or even if you do, but you haven't been included in their golden circle), you may be happier concentrating on finding a few special friends you enjoy and who like you—whether you make mistakes or are having an "off" day or wear plaid.

These are friends with whom you can share secrets and dreams and private thoughts. These are friends worth having. Maybe you'll find them individually in classes or in school activities. Maybe you'll meet them outside of school. Maybe you'll come to know them as you mingle in a group of classmates with whom you feel comfortable.

You may not only be happy outside the in-group, but you may be *happier* as you discover some real friends, people who really want your friendship and think you're special for all the right reasons.

If the Cliques at Your School Make Breaking Into the Activities You Most Enjoy Impossible Or Making Friends Very Difficult, Start Discovering Friendships Outside of School. This doesn't mean that you're condemned to eating lunch alone every school day forever more. If you participate in church activities, in community theater, scouting, or volunteer work, you may get to know some people at your school *outside* of their cliques and in an atmosphere that makes friendship easier. This friendship may then carry over to school. Or you may meet someone from school who isn't in a clique, but whom you might not have known except for this shared outside interest. That, too, can be a good beginning for a new friendship. And even if you don't meet people from your school in these outside settings, these activities can help you to feel good about yourself *and* make friends who bring you support, comfort, and pleasure outside of school.

Discover and Appreciate Your Own Special Qualities—Even If These Don't Match the In-Group's Traits. Remember that the "givens" that can mean admission to the in-group—like great looks, a winning smile, great clothes, parental money or position—can be taken away or fade with time. Some of the qualities, too, don't mean as much when people are more mature and look for deeper, more lasting qualities in friendships and love relationships.

The promise of better times to come in adulthood may be scant comfort right now when you're feeling rejected, but discovering and appreciating the qualities that make you special can start improving your life *today.*

Are you kind? Are you sensitive to the feelings of others? Do you feel deeply? Are you intelligent or talented in some way that brings you joy? Are you creative? Are you a good friend? Do you listen? Do you have a sense of humor? Do you have compassion for others? Do you have a lively interest in new people and new ideas?

All of these qualities—and many more—are ones that can enrich your life now and for many years to come.

Think of your good qualities and accept the fact that, whether or not you have a lot of friends, whether or not others at school consider you IN, you're a good, worthwhile person.

Amazingly, this quiet self-acceptance can clue others in that you're a person worth knowing. If you're self-accepting, you will no longer walk around with downcast eyes or put yourself down (before someone else gets around to it) or brand yourself as a loser. When you accept yourself as the imperfect, but very special person you are, others will begin to accept and like you, too.

You may not be the most powerful person in school. You may not be the most popular. But you will have friendships worth having. And you will have the freedom and the joy of being yourself.

MY GRADES ARE A PROBLEM

Until this year, my grades have always been great. I've made mostly "A's" and a few "B's." Now, in junior high, I'm making mostly "C's," and my parents are ready to ground me for the rest of the year. I don't know what's wrong. Sometimes I have trouble concentrating. But I haven't been goofing off. What can I do?

Mark L.

What do you do if you make good grades and nobody likes you because of this? I have a few friends, who are considered "brains" like me, but I've never had a date—and most girls in my class (the eighth grade) already have boyfriends. My parents are happy about my grades, but they're the only ones.

Melanie G.

My grades aren't as good as they could be. I do my homework just fine. I understand my classes. My problem is that I panic during tests and don't do well. So my grades aren't great. What can I do?

Lisa D.

I used to do well in school, but I'm so bored, I can hardly stand it. The teachers are boring. The classes are boring. I'm in eighth grade, so I can't exactly drop out of school. My folks are giving me a hard time about my falling grades. Also, they're worried that I might be depressed or on drugs because my grades are dropping. But that's not it at all. I'm just totally bored. What can I do?

Greg A.

I've always had trouble in school. Now it looks like I have some learning disability. I'm supposed to take special classes. But I don't want to take special ed because my friends will call me a "retard."

Joe W.

Grades can be a special challenge when everyone expects so much of you—and when you're busy adjusting to a new school. Or they can be a challenge in a different way when you get "A's," but find that it isn't considered cool to get good grades at your school. Boredom can also hit hard when it seems like you've been in school forever—and have so many years left to go. And a learning disability can be especially painful when it's discovered at a time when you don't want to be different—or be treated in a different way—from your friends.

What can you do if you find yourself experiencing an academic crisis?

IF YOUR GRADES HAVE FALLEN AND YOU DON'T KNOW WHY

It could be that you're devoting more energy right now to adjusting to junior high or your physical changes. It isn't at all unusual for people in their early teens to have a temporary drop in grades when they're busy dealing with all these changes.

Are your grades going down for all your classes—or just one or two classes?

If it's just one class that's a problem, think hard and talk it over with your parents or teacher and try to figure out why. Ask for help. Or look for a special circumstance. For example, it's not unusual for girls, once they get in junior high, to start faltering in math and science, even though they may have excelled in these subjects in elementary school. Quite often, this is because doing well in these so-called "masculine" fields seems suddenly unfeminine, and a girl, maybe without realizing it, may develop a sudden fear, lack of confidence, or lack of interest in these subjects.

No interests or classes are "masculine" or "feminine" and, especially if you've always done well in math or science and suddenly have problems, you may need some special encouragement from parents, teachers, and *yourself* that it's okay to be good in these areas.

If all of your grades are falling, even after you're used to the school and are feeling fairly uncomfortable with your own changes, ask yourself what *else* has been happening in your life in the past year or so. Family problems, a parental divorce, illness, the death of someone close. . . . all of these things can take your energy and attention away from your studies. If this might be the problem, look for ways to resolve your feelings. Talk with friends or family members. Seek help from a teacher or clergyperson or some other adult you feel you can trust. You don't have to go on suffering—and neither do your grades. When you start feeling better, you'll regain your confidence in your studies, too.

IF YOU'RE MAKING GOOD GRADES AND LOSING FRIENDS

Some people fear that being labeled a "brain" (or worse, a "drudge" or a "nerd") means instant unpopularity, no dates ever, and lunchtime loneliness into the next century.

It's true that many kids look up to athletes and down at scholars. It's true that some very insecure guys feel threatened by smart girls. Some tease classmates who actually study during study hall and always hand in homework on time.

The answer to all this is NOT to cave in to pressure to goof off and be less than your best academically. You owe it to yourself, first, to be the best you can be. You can do that and still have friends, dates, and lunch companions—really!

How?

Don't Try to Play Dumb. It's a phony act. Everyone will know it—and they'll resent you for it. It's better to use your energy to go on doing your best—and to find friends who will accept you as you are.

Be Aware of Ways You Might Be Using Your Intelligence to Keep Others Away. Do you feel that your total value as a person lies in your grades? If so, you may talk about them too much or, without realizing it, fall into the pattern of constantly comparing your grades to those of others so you can keep feeling superior. Do you show off your knowledge around people you know are having trouble in school or who really can't fully appreciate what you're discussing? Bragging about your achievements or flaunting your intelligence around people who can't keep up with you will build a wall of resentment between you and others. You can be proud of your achievements and accept your intelligence as an important part of yourself without making other people feel stupid. There is a big difference between using your intelligence to help a classmate who's having trouble understanding class material and using your special abilities in a show-off fashion meant to make that person feel even more inferior.

Accept Other People As They Are. Some academically bright people lose friends—or valuable opportunities for friendship—because they think that there's only one way to be smart. That isn't true. Every person is special. And there are many different kinds of intelligence. It takes a special gift to be able to dance well or excel at a sport. It takes a special kind of intelligence to build good relationships, to be sensitive to others' feelings, to know when to give and when to take. Some people have one kind of intelligence but are average in other ways. Some people seem to shine in all ways. But don't assume that someone isn't worth knowing just because he or she doesn't have good grades or high aspirations. There are all kinds of ways to be a success.

When you can see and take pleasure in other people's successes *of all kinds,* when you can let people know that you appreciate their special qualities, they will be more likely to admire yours—and to like you.

Give Your Classmates Time to Grow Up a Little. Bright girls especially need to know this. The guys who are most likely to be threatened by a girl who is smart are those who are insecure. Sometimes boys, who develop a little more slowly than girls in junior high, try to hide this insecurity by acting super-macho and feel like they have to be in charge of everything in a relationship. So they may avoid a girl who is obviously bright or more mature. In time, as they grow and mature, some of these guys will change their views. In the meantime, make friends with guys a little older than you are—maybe a ninth grader if you're in seventh or eighth grade. Look for guys who also do well and who feel good about themselves. A man who feels secure and good about himself will be most likely to enjoy—rather than reject—you.

IF YOU SUFFER FROM EXAM JITTERS

Most people feel a little anxious before exams, but some get so nervous that they never test well—and so their grades don't reflect their real abilities.

What can you do if you're in this spot?

Tell Yourself That You'll Survive—No Matter What! Lots of people make themselves unbelievably nervous by saying, when they're going into a test, "If I don't get a good grade on this (or if I don't pass this), that's IT!"

When you feel your whole future hinges on one test, you're going to panic. And that doesn't do anything for your test-taking ability.

Even if you don't do well on this test, you will survive. No one is really going to kill you because you make a less-than-perfect score or grade. You or your parents may be disappointed if you don't do well, but you'll survive. Even if the test is a one-of-a-kind sort of thing, like an entrance exam to a private school, the test isn't everything. Knowing that some people test better than others, admissions officials also look at general class grades, school activities, and the general impression you give them during the entrance interview. And even if you blow the test so completely that you don't get into that school, you're still going to go to some school. You may be disappointed for a while, but you'll be fine.

If you can go into an important exam saying to yourself, "No matter what happens with this, I'll be fine," you'll be better able to relax and do your best.

Listen to Or Read All the Instructions. Don't get so busy worrying that you don't listen to important directions. Read any instructions on the exam itself. This can keep you from making confidence-shaking mistakes and can get you off to a good start. (This can also give you a little more time to calm down before actually beginning the test.)

If Possible, Read Over the Test Before Beginning. This isn't always possible with a timed objective test, but if this is an exam with a lot of essay questions, it makes sense to read over it first. Many times, your answer to one question may suggest an answer or approach to another one.

Answer the Easy Questions First. This will help your confidence to grow as you get into the test. It will give you a sense of success *and* more time to think about the hard questions!

Do a Relaxation Exercise When You Start to Tense Up. Don't let tension take over. Stop momentarily, close your eyes and breathe deeply. Relax your shoulders, your neck, and your stomach muscles. Breathe deeply again. And remind yourself that, no matter what happens with this one test, you'll be fine. You will have many, many chances for success in your life.

IF YOU HAVE A LEARNING DISABILITY OR NEED SPECIAL ED

It can hurt when other people make fun of you, but what matters most is that you're getting the special help you need. Don't become a willing victim and let others know that their jeers are getting to you.

Remember that refusing special ed help at this point may mean that you go through school feeling like a failure and never catch up. Some teasing from so-called friends isn't nearly as awful as going through the next few years feeling like a total failure. Your need for special ed may be temporary or only for a few subjects. With this special help, you'll be fine. You'll learn what you need to learn. You'll overcome or be better able to cope with a special learning problem. You'll graduate. And that's a major success!

IF YOU'RE TOO BORED TO CARE

Maybe you're tired of working so hard in classes that have little, if anything, to do with your real interests.

Maybe you're so uninterested in your classes that it's hard to listen or study without your mind wandering.

Maybe you're bright and bored—and your classes have stopped being a challenge.

Maybe you're just bored with life in general.

Boredom can be very tiring—and it makes you less able to pursue activities that *might* interest you.

So what can you do to get rid of your boredom—even though you're stuck in the same old school with the same old boring classes with all those boring teachers?

Concentrate on Areas of Life That Don't Bore You. Is there a hobby or special interest you really enjoy? Do it! Maybe it's an extra-curricular activity at school, or sports, drama, dance, or music outside of school. Maybe it's a religious commitment or an interest in volunteer work. Whatever makes you feel more alive and energetic, do it! Concentrate on improving your friendships—and enjoy the results.

These activities can all lift your spirits so much that school may seem less boring all of a sudden. When you're active and involved, you feel like being *more* active. You get new ideas and new enthusiasm.

Look for New Challenges. If you're bright and bored by class material—go beyond it.

Take enrichment courses if these are available. Take special summer courses for gifted students. Go to an arts camp or a computer camp. Learn a new skill.

Or study something on your own. Take a topic from class and, instead of skimming the surface the way the class does, learn everything you can about it. For example, you might do your own research project on a figure from history. If your class has been studying World War II, for example, do some reading on the side about a major figure from that time. Go to the library and listen to a tape of President Roosevelt's or Winston Churchill's speeches. Rent a video documentary from that time period. Or learn about someone who was very important then, but who is less known now. For instance, after your class studies all about Adolf Hitler, do some research on your own to find out who Albert Speer was, why he was very important to Germany, and how he was different from other Nazi leaders. Or pursue one of your own interests—from dinosaurs to black holes to the history of rock—entirely on your own time. If you're sick to death of writing boring essays for English class (like what you did on your summer vacation), write something just for yourself. Keep a journal where you can write the thoughts, feelings, and experiences important to *you*. Or write a poem or short story just for the fun of it!

Make Time for Fun. If your life is just studying, studying, and more studying—no wonder you're bored! Fun, friends, and physical activity are important to feeling interested and alive. Yes, studying is important. But make time for these other vital parts of life, too. It will be time well spent.

Don't Look for Meaning—Look for Opportunities—in Your Classes. As you struggle through algebra or medieval history or Latin I or a tome like *Beowulf,* you may wonder what meaning this could possibly have in your life today and in your life to come.

Well, guess what? Maybe it has *no* real meaning for you now or ever.

But even the most boring class can be an opportunity. It can be an opportunity to develop discipline as you learn to listen to and study material that is somewhat less than fascinating.

You may find this discipline useful in the near future when you need to be extra patient in listening to a friend whose problem you may find a bit boring, but who needs you nonetheless.

Later on, this can be useful when you're working. Part-time student jobs, like those at fast-food restaurants, aren't exactly a thrill a minute, but the more discipline you have the better. And even later on, your career, even if you like it a lot, isn't always going to be fascinating. (Even movie stars have boring times of waiting around, sometimes for *hours*, on the set!)

And you don't always know what's going to be useful in the future. Some people claim, looking back, that the classes they thought were the least helpful at the time were the *most* helpful later on. So you never know.

Another opportunity that your classes can give you is to open your mind and expand your view of things. Maybe a teacher bores you because you disagree with his or her view of things. Stop and think about that. In trying to discover why this person holds these views, what merit there may be in them (even though you continue to disagree), and what *other* ways there may be of looking at this subject, you can give your mind valuable exercise and experience. Learning to hear and think about all points of view, even if they seem boring or silly to you, can help you to grow as a person in wonderful new ways!

TEACHER TROUBLE

My math teacher hurts my feelings all the time because he says I'm stupid right in front of the class! I cry whenever I think about this. What can I do?

Jennifer J.

I have this brilliant older brother. All the teachers expect me to be like him. When I'm not, they make a big deal about it. My English teacher is especially bad about this. She's always going on and on about Brian and how great he was and how she can't understand why I can't be more like him. It's depressing!

Brad L.

I got caught cheating earlier this year. This one teacher won't forget about it. Most people cheat at one time or another. I just got caught. But now this teacher watches me like I was a criminal! He constantly picks on me and blames me for any trouble in class. How can I change his mind about me?

Russ G.

I have a problem: I like my social studies teacher too much! I think of him all the time and dream about us getting married someday. He's 24 years old and looks like he could be on TV. He isn't married. He's very nice to me and I think he likes me, but it hasn't been any more than that, except in my mind. What can I do? (My friend Patti has an even worse problem: She has a crush on the gym teacher, who's a woman. Does this mean something is wrong with her, if you know what I mean?)

Julie A.

Teacher trouble can happen for a lot of different reasons. Maybe you create a lot of it for yourself by clowning around or otherwise disrupting the class. Or maybe you put your teacher on the spot by constantly challenging his or her authority or criticizing him or her in front of the class.

There are teachers who spell trouble, too. Not all of them are fair, kind, or competent. Sometimes they make mistakes—like when they label you "stupid" or compare you unfairly to a sibling, a friend, or another student. Sometimes they need more information in order to know and trust you, especially if you have a history (deserved or not) of causing problems in class.

What can you do if you have teacher trouble?

The best way to handle teacher trouble is to decide whose problem it is.

Some teachers are cranky, unlikely to change, and can be lived with only if you keep from aggravating them as much as possible.

If you're feeling bad because a teacher is labeling you "stupid" or comparing you unfavorably to someone else or picking on you because of something that happened a long time ago, this is a problem for you. And the best way to deal with that problem is to ask for your teacher's help.

Why would you do this—when, from your point of view, your teacher is wrong?

Think about it. If you go up to a teacher and say, "You're wrong to do that!" you may get a quick trip to the principal's office and invite even more intense teacher trouble. But if you go to the teacher privately and quietly, and respectfully tell him or her what your feelings are, how you are affected by something he/she has said or does, and ask for the teacher's help in some way, you'll be much more likely to resolve your teacher trouble.

How does this work in real life?

Jennifer might go to the teacher who calls her "stupid" and tell him, in private: "I feel really embarrassed and upset when you call me 'stupid.' I'm losing confidence and this makes it even harder to do my best. I really want to do better. Can you help me?"

If her teacher is a decent person who just lost his temper, he may be very willing to help and may apologize for hurting her feelings.

But it's possible that the teacher has a problem that has very little to do with Jennifer. Maybe he feels inadequate himself and gets a special sense of power by making students feel helpless and miserable. Maybe he thinks girls are, by nature, deficient in math. Maybe making fun of students is such a habit that nothing Jennifer says is going to make any difference. Maybe the teacher is a jerk.

If that's the case, Jennifer is going to have to look to others—other teachers, parents, relatives, friends and, most important, *herself* for words of encouragement. She can begin to see this labeling as her *teacher's* problem, as his inability to see her potential, and then separate herself from that unfair label.

This doesn't mean that being called "stupid" won't hurt. It will. She will probably remember this hurt for a very long time. But Jennifer (and you, too, if you have a similar problem) can try to take in as little of that hurt as possible, telling herself that no teacher can know her as well as *she* does—and she knows, deep down, that she isn't stupid.

Many famous, successful people—like the mathematical genius Albert Einstein and the incredible inventor Thomas Edison—were considered hopeless failures by some of their teachers and happily went on to prove them wrong.

Many others who have survived teacher labeling may not be famous, but are happy and successful in their lives and their own ways. You can be, too, no matter *what* this teacher says!

If a teacher compares you unfairly to someone else, like Brad's teacher who compares him with his brilliant older brother, it may help to tell the teacher, quietly and in private, "I feel hurt when I'm constantly compared to my older brother. He's great. I'm really proud of his accomplishments. But I'm a different person. I have different abilities. When I'm compared to Brian, it makes it very hard for me to do my best."

And if a teacher has had it in for you because of past trouble, a quiet talk may also help. You might start off by saying something like, "I understand, because of past problems, that you want to keep an eye on me. But I feel sometimes that I get blamed for things I didn't do. I want very much for you to trust me again. If you give me a chance, I'll show you that I *can* be trusted!" (And then put all your best efforts into proving yourself right!)

What if you are in love with or have a crush on a teacher?

That's very common at this time of life—and it can be a special emotional learning experience, too.

Having the experience of loving someone from afar, someone who because of age and position is really not available to you romantically, helps you to learn what it means to love someone outside your family. (And if a teacher *is* seductive to you, if he or she is aware of your feelings and uses these as an excuse to become romantically involved with you, this is not love on his or her part, but exploitation. It is wrong for an adult to take advantage of your loving feelings in a sexual way.) A teacher who really cares about you—and who has guessed or been told the way you feel—will say "No" to seductive possibilities while encouraging you to grow as a person.

Having a crush on a teacher may mean that you are ready to feel love, but not to *do* anything about these loving feelings. So you fall in love with someone you can't have—whether that is a teacher or a favorite rock, TV, or movie star. Later, when you're feeling ready for actual romantic involvement, chances are you'll find yourself falling in love with someone closer to your own age and experience, someone who is, theoretically, available to you.

In the meantime, these feelings of love and admiration for a teacher can simply be enjoyed for what they are: new, intense feelings that can bring both pleasure and pain. You don't need to tell anyone—least of all, the teacher. You don't need to act on these feelings. You can simply learn, from these beginnings, some of the joy and frustration that loving someone can bring.

If you find yourself loving or intensely admiring a teacher of the same sex, this is normal, too. This is a time when you're trying to separate a bit from your parents. So you may find yourself looking up to other adults to admire and imitate—and teachers, many of them quite admirable people, are the outside-the-family adults you're most likely to encounter. Feeling love for a same-sex adult friend or, for that matter, for a best girlfriend or male buddy is an important part of learning to love and accept yourself as a male or as a female. For example, girls who say, "Oh, I can't really be close to other girls. They bore me. I prefer guys," are rejecting themselves in emotionally rejecting those of the same sex.

We need to value and love our families and people outside our families—and friends of both sexes. This really has nothing to do with sex or romantic love (even when a crush includes romantic or sexual fantasies)—and everything to do with becoming a happy, loving, self-accepting person.

Finding a special teacher of either sex to love and admire can help you to discover and strengthen your good feelings about yourself—and your ability to love another.

MAKING A NEW START

I didn't do so good in school up to now. My family moved a lot, so I went to three different grade schools and it was hard. Now we've bought a house. It's in the town where my grandparents live and I think we'll stay. I'll be starting junior high soon. I want to do better from now on. How can I do this?

Jeremy C.

My parents keep telling me how important it is for me to do well now that I'm in eighth grade. My grades have never been especially good. I'm not good about doing homework or understanding stuff in class right away. I'm embarrassed to ask questions or for special help. I'm scared of looking stupid. What can I do to make things different in my new school?

Terri S.

Now that I'm in junior high, my parents say I have to be responsible. They say I have to get my homework and chores done without them standing there making me do them. But they still nag me. And this makes me not want to do anything. How can I get them off my case?

Christopher M.

Junior high can be a wonderful new beginning. If you didn't do as well as you might have or had poor study habits before, you can start over. If you have always been a good student but are worried about harder classes, the higher expectations of teachers and parents, and more competition from classmates now that you're in junior high, a change in your habits and your attitude about homework and school can give you new confidence.

What can you do if you're feeling overwhelmed by the new challenges of your junior high classes?

- Pay attention! When you listen as carefully as you can in class (even if the teacher is boring), you may hear new facts that help a subject begin to make sense to you. Listening can also give you clues about what the teacher thinks is important (and what will probably appear in upcoming exams). And listening will help you to ask more intelligent, to-the-point questions in class. (Listening will also spare you the horrible embarrassment of having a private fantasy interrupted by a question from the teacher that is so far from your train of thought that it might as well be in a foreign language.)

Learn to take notes on key facts and important information and issues. This will help you to understand class material better or to discover what you need to have explained over again.

- If you don't understand something, say so. You won't be alone. The sooner you ask, the better off you'll be. Lots of people are scared to ask a teacher to repeat an explanation or make it clearer—and so they go on and on not understanding. It's likely that a number of your classmates also don't understand, but are too embarrassed to speak up. They'll be glad you did and won't consider you stupid. Asking for help early on will get you off to a good start. If you don't, you'll only get more confused and overwhelmed.
- If you're struggling with a subject, ask for special help. Again, the earlier you do this, the better. Meet with your teacher privately and ask for help. Or get together

with a parent or even a friend who has special expertise in this subject. Ask your parents if you can get some tutoring.

This help isn't meant to replace your own hard work. Shortcuts like having your friend (or a parent) do your homework for you isn't the answer. You may never be great at this subject, but you *can* do better with help and hard work.

Knowing when you need extra help—and asking for it—is smart.

• Make good use of extra moments at school. If you think about it, you'll find that you have lots of little moments before classes begin or during study hall or while waiting for a friend to join you for lunch to sneak in some study. Review class notes, language flash cards, or vocabulary lists. Spend *some* time going over class material with a friend. This doesn't mean being a total drudge or, even worse, a hermit. It just means getting some studying done during boring moments of waiting so that you will either get more studying done with less pain, *or* get more of your studying done during school so you'll have less to do *after* school.

If homework has been a hassle, what can you do to get it done without having your parents nagging you every minute?

• Find a good place and time to study. This may seem pretty basic, but it's important! Maybe you've been having trouble getting your homework done because you've been trying to do it in front of the television set or so late at night (or early in the morning) that you're too tired to concentrate. If you like studying with some background noise, turn on the radio—softly. If you need privacy, do your homework in your room *during a set time* each evening. If you like to be around people, but need quiet, do your homework at the local library or at a time when a sibling is also studying or your parents are engaged in quiet activities like reading or sewing.

Think of the best possible study atmosphere and time for you and then stick to it.

Plan on setting aside several hours each school night for studying—whether or not you have that much homework on a given night. You can use the extra time to review all your class notes or do assigned reading or start long-term projects (like reports or term papers).

• Don't make studying cruel and unusual punishment. If you decide you're going to spend three hours on one subject tonight, chances are you'll get bored, frustrated, and stop concentrating long before that time limit is up. When your mind starts to wander, take a break. Study something else for a while and come back to the first subject later.

Reward yourself in little ways. When you've finished doing the homework for your hardest or least favorite subject, go right on to your favorite subject. Or take a break from studying for ten minutes to listen to a favorite song or exercise or talk. Or get all your studying done so you can watch your favorite TV show as a reward.

If you make studying a punishment, you'll resent it and find it harder and harder to work.

• Plan ahead. That's a very important growing-up skill to learn. We all have times when we start a project late and end up doing most of it the night before it's due. But if that's your usual pattern, you're making school harder for yourself than it has to be.

Get a calendar/assignment book with lots of space to make notes. Then, when you have a report or paper assigned for next week, next month, or the end of the semester, plan how you will do this in little stages so it won't become this horrible thing you're dreading and end up working on for twenty-four hours straight the day before it's due. You might decide to have the research done by a certain date. Then start writing it on a certain date . . . and plan it step by step from there so that you can finish on time or ahead of time. You'll be amazed how good it will feel when *you* take charge of your time and your projects! Far from being a drudge, you'll have even more time for fun (without having the dread of a project left undone hanging over your head).

• Keep your studies separate from hassles with your parents. It can be tempting to make schoolwork and grades the stage for fighting with your parents. After all, it really gets to them when you're smart and yet don't achieve. It really gets their attention when your grades drop all of a sudden. And it can be tempting, the more they want you to excel, to dig in your heels and exert your individuality by doing the opposite.

But the person who gets hurt the most by all of this is *you*!

Take responsibility for doing your homework and then *do* it. That will keep your parents from nagging you.

If you feel like rebelling, show your differences in ways that won't hurt you or your future. Express your thoughts, feelings, and ideas in your own way. Dress in your own way. Decide which values are most important to you. There are all kinds of ways to be your own person without creating more problems for yourself.

And, if you've been using trouble at school to let your parents know that you're hurting, please realize that there are better ways to ask for help and reassurance. Tell your parents or other people close to you when you're feeling bad, instead of letting a grade slump go on and on. People will be there to help if you ask in a more direct way. And you'll feel better sooner.

Some young people think that studying, doing homework and handing it in on time, and listening in class is like being a child simply going along with adults. But that isn't true.

Mature people do what they need to do—even when they don't feel like doing it.

Mature people know that there is a time for work and a time for fun, and both are important in our lives.

Mature people plan ahead and take charge of their time so that they'll be able to do not only what they have to do, but things they really *want* to do.

Right now, today, in junior high, you can take an important step toward becoming your own mature, responsible, and fun-loving person!

CHAPTER FOUR

How to Tell a Friend from an Enemy (and How to Be a Good Friend)

How do you know if someone is a friend or an enemy? I have this best friend I'll call "Cece." Sometimes we're really close, then she ignores me. Then we're close again and we tell each other EVERYTHING. Then she'll spread my secrets all over school. I don't know whether she's a real friend because she acts a lot like an enemy. But still, she's the best friend I've got!

Tracy K.

Sometimes, as Tracy points out, it *is* hard to tell a friend from an enemy.

Friends can be impatient or critical. They can disappoint you.

There are times, too, when someone you haven't liked, someone you know could never be a close friend, surprises you with an unexpected kindness.

Then there are times when people who were once friends become enemies, times when a treasured friendship vanishes into silent hurt and angry feelings.

Friends are so important to you now that it's vital to be able to tell a friend from an enemy, to know how to make and *keep* friends, how to nurture a friendship through good times and bad times, and how to know when it's time to let go of a friendship.

HOW TO FIT IN AND MAKE FRIENDS

How do you go about making friends when you don't have any? It seems like I don't fit in with any group, and nobody notices me. I try to be a good listener, but it doesn't work. I just stand there not being noticed.

"Lonely"

84

How can I make friends at a school where I can't find anyone who is like me? I'm very interested in politics and the environment and things like that, and nobody else seems to care. What can I do?

John W.

I'm really good at sharing my feelings and all. I'm real open and can talk about anything. But it's getting where people avoid me. Why don't I have any real friends if I can talk about feelings and all the things friends are supposed to talk about?

Annelise Q.

Not having friends can be painful and puzzling, especially if you're really trying to listen and communicate well with others.

And it can feel pretty lonely if you find that you don't seem to have much in common with the people in your class, yet you can't imagine going to school day after day without any special friends.

If you're not fitting in and making friends, how can you start changing this? You might start by asking yourself the following questions:

- Am I reaching out to others—or am I waiting for someone to come to me? If you sit around waiting for a best friend to come your way, you may wait a long time! If you want to have friends, you need to let people know. A lot of people are shy and fear rejection—just like you do at times. Someone has to take the risk and say "Hello" first. Someone has to suggest sitting together at lunch first. Someone has to start that first conversation. Why shouldn't it be you?
- Am I too busy being right to make friends? Some people are so intent on winning that they lose the opportunity to make friends. If you have a need to be right all the time, if you think your opinions are the only right ones, if you're judgmental about other people's feelings, you may be turning other people off. You don't have to agree with someone to be his or her friend. You don't have to deny your opinions. But, if you want to have friends, you need to develop tolerance for other points of view and the compassion and wisdom to know when to shut up. You can have some beautiful friendships with people whose views and life experiences are quite different from yours. If you treasure these friendships, you'll be wise to leave each other alone in the areas where you'll never agree and, instead, enjoy what you *do* share with each other.
- Am I listening too hard and contributing too little to conversations? Being a good listener *is* an admirable quality. But a truly good listener doesn't just stand there nodding, blending in with the wallpaper. A good listener asks questions. A good listener helps the other person feel smart. A good listener also contributes to the conversation.

Some experts claim that you can win friends by listening and showing interest in what they're saying. Others claim that you need to be an interesting person yourself. The real secret to being noticed and liked by others is a combination of the two. You need to develop your interests, your point of view, your good feelings about yourself. You need to do what you love to do and be with people you truly enjoy. And it does help to listen, to help others to feel important and liked. If you can combine interest in others with your own growth as a fascinating person, you'll make some wonderful friendships.

- Am I coming on too strong too soon? Friendships evolve over time as you build trust and become more comfortable with one another. If you tell someone your life history, including very painful, private things, as soon as you meet, the other person may feel overwhelmed or embarrassed and pull away.

   Your feelings are tender. Don't expose them to someone you don't know well and trust. Sharing daily activities and little secrets at first may help you build a friendship to a point where you *can* tell each other everything—or almost everything. But that doesn't happen overnight.

   If you come on strong and try to take over another person's life and time—making plans to spend *all* your free time together—you may also drive a potential friend away. Remember, this person needs time to get used to you. This person probably also has other friends and other demands on his or her time, and, as you get to know one another, you'll naturally begin to fit into each other's lives without either one of you getting the sense that the other person is trying to take over completely.

- Do I share who I am with people who care? There are all kinds of friendships. Some are activity-oriented: You get together just to go skating or play squash or study for a French exam but otherwise you don't have much in common. Some friendships go far beyond activities to sharing feelings. Are you really letting people know you? Some people are so busy trying to look perfect to their friends that they don't see that they're pushing them away with this perfection. Friends like each other and feel close for a lot of reasons, including shared embarrassments, problems, and uncertainties. When you can share these troubled as well as happy feelings with someone, you are on the way to building a close and special friendship.

WHO IS A FRIEND?

A friend is someone who:
- can be happy for you as well as sad for you, someone who is as glad to hear your good news as he or she is supportive when you have bad news;
- sees you as an equal, who doesn't insist on your giving in and doing only what he or she wants, all the time;
- is loyal, someone who cares about you in good times and bad times, someone who won't turn on you, betray you, or make fun of your most tender or private feelings;
- keeps your secrets, the small ones and the big ones, someone who would break a confidence only to save your life. If someone is suicidal and can't or won't get help, it is an act of love for a friend to let adult people who can help know about this;
- gives as well as takes, someone who is as happy to listen to your feelings and problems as he or she is to talk about his or her own;

- respects your feelings and point of view, even when you disagree;
- is not only fun to be with, but *comfortable* to be with. When you are comfortable in a friendship, you don't have to talk constantly or have riotous fun all the time. Quiet times and ordinary times can be very special, too, when you're with a good friend;
- realizes that you need time—and other friends—of your own. A good friendship doesn't mean you have to be together constantly, though you may choose to spend a lot of your free time together. You can enjoy times apart and the company of others. You don't have to have all the same friends, the same interests, or the same tastes. There is room in your relationship for your individual differences. And even though you enjoy being together, you don't have to be. You can spend a day, a week, or a summer apart and pick up right where you left off;
- keeps promises to you whenever possible. If your friend says she'll sit with you on the bus during the field trip, she'll be there and won't disappoint you at the last minute. If, for some reason, this arrangement won't work out, she'll let you know why—in advance—and maybe help you to find another seatmate;
- won't walk away the minute the going gets tough between you. No one is perfect. Loving, caring friends can still irritate, anger, and disappoint each other. But they know that the friendship is more important than the problems . . . and they work through these, have the courage to say "I'm sorry," and forgive each other countless times.

WHO IS AN ENEMY?

An enemy is someone who:
- makes a habit of hurting you. This person steps on your feelings, sabotages your love relationships, tries to make you think that your talents and accomplishments don't count for much, and generally makes you miserable. Not everyone is an obvious enemy. Some people get to you with little comments tacked on to what are supposed to be compliments or make you feel bad with all kinds of advice they claim is just for your own good. But if you're feeling bad every time you are with this person, you may have an enemy, not a friend!
- encourages you to share secrets just so he or she can get another news bulletin to spread around school (and look important);
- wants to be a friend just in order to get something from you. Maybe you have a brother (or sister) he or she would like to date. Maybe you have homework this person always wants to copy. You get the idea. The tip-off: When this person gets what he or she wants from you, he doesn't want to know you—until the next time he needs something;
- sets you up to be embarrassed. If you have a so-called "friend" who makes you the butt of all his/her jokes or who acts totally different when you're with other people, then what you have here may not be a friend;
- doesn't consider or give any importance to your feelings, even when you express them directly. If you let this person know that you feel bad when she embarrasses you or tells your secrets or tries to get your boyfriend to like her instead . . . and she (or he) doesn't listen or care or do anything to change this hurtful behavior, it may be time to admit to yourself that this is not a friendship—and move on to

people who will really care about you as the special person you are and the wonderful friend you can be.

COPING WITH THE DOWN TIMES OF FRIENDSHIP

I really like my best friend a lot. So why am I so nasty to her sometimes? If a teacher yells at me or me and my mom had a fight before school, I start taking out my bad mood on my friend. I'm scared of losing her and don't know how to stop this.

Jessica D.

There is this girl I like as a friend. But it really bugs me when she gets a better grade than I do in a test or a class. One of the things I like about her so much is that she's smart, but when she does better than I do, I get mad and avoid her. I know this hurts her and I don't mean to. I guess I feel fairly competitive with her even though she's my friend. Does this make me a bad friend?

Tom S.

I know my best friend cares about me, but it makes me want to lie down and DIE when she goes around asking guys if they like me and trying to get someone to ask me out! I really want to have a boyfriend, but I'd rather have a boy get the idea he likes me all on his own instead of her dragging him over to me. How can I tell her to stop trying to get me a boyfriend without hurting her feelings?

Megan O.

My best friend, Cindy, says that since I have a boyfriend, I don't have time for her anymore. We don't spend as much time together, but I still like her as a best friend. How do I find time for her so we can stay friends and still have a boyfriend? She doesn't date yet and she doesn't think much of my boyfriend.

Jana W.

Friendships are a wonderful part of life. But they're not always easy.

We can be competitive with friends and mean to friends, and they can be the same to us.

We can embarrass or hurt each other without really meaning to.

And sometimes a friend can look quite a lot like an enemy.

But there is a difference between a friendship that is going through a down time and a real adversary relationship.

The main difference: Friends regret being mean or hurting each other and try not to do it again. Friends worry about whether it's okay to feel competitive sometimes and work hard not to let competitive feelings harm the caring between them. Your feelings matter to a friend. So if you tell her that she has hurt you, she will apologize and make a real effort not to do that again.

An enemy, on the other hand, doesn't care that you've been hurt or really *meant* to hurt you. To a nonfriend, what you're feeling doesn't matter.

So, when you care and yet you find your friendship with someone going through a down time, read through some of the following situations. Perhaps they may be helpful to you.

If you find yourself taking out your anger on an innocent friend (or he or she is doing this to you):

This can happen because the angry person feels safe enough with the friend to show anger and knows that the other person will understand and forgive.

But you can't always count on that. If you constantly turn on a friend when you're really angry at a teacher or a parent or someone else in your class, that friend may start to wonder if this relationship is worth the trouble. And it doesn't do you any good either. When you're mean to others, you may start to feel like a terrible person. But you're not a terrible person. You just need to learn to handle your anger in a way that doesn't hurt yourself and the people who matter to you.

Find new ways to deal with pent-up anger and frustration: Take a walk, exercise in some other way, write in your diary, talk to your friend about the person or situation upsetting you and ask for suggestions. That will do a lot more for your friendship and your self-esteem.

If you have a friend who dumps bad feelings on *you,* let him or her know how this affects you. While friends forgive each other and stand by each other through all kinds of troubles, this commitment doesn't give one friend the right to abuse another. Let your friend know that you care and that you're there to listen and help, but that you won't allow him or her to make you a victim. Suggest taking a walk, exercising together, or talking. Stand up for yourself while showing concern for the other person.

If a friend and your dating life are somehow at odds:

Friends can be wonderfully supportive when it comes to dating: They can fix you up with people, listen to your happy feelings, and help ease your pain in a breakup. But sometimes complications arise.

If you have a friend like Megan's, someone who is driving you crazy and embarrassing you to death while trying to liven up your social life, tell her that you really appreciate her concern for you, but that you would rather handle those details yourself. You might explain to her that you get embarrassed when you see people being pressured, perhaps, to meet you and like you. Tell her that you would like the slow, natural process of getting to know, like, and maybe even love someone. Praise her as a friend and tell her that it means a lot to have a friend who cares so much, but that you would prefer that she show her caring in other ways.

If you have a friend who ignores you the minute she gets a boyfriend and who spends what little time you do have together talking about him incessantly, you'll also need to speak up. You might say something like, "I feel hurt when you more or less ignore me every time you're going with someone. I know your boyfriend is important to you and I'm happy for you. But I miss you. I feel I'm losing you as a special friend when we rarely see each other and when we do, you talk only about *him* and not about *you.* I would like to have some time together again when we can just enjoy each other."

If you've been ignoring a friend in favor of a date, keep in mind that just because you're in love doesn't mean that you don't need your separate friends. Having your own life and your own friends can bring a balance to your lives and your relationship. Make time for friends. They're important. A friendship may endure long after a dating relationship is history. So don't let falling in love overshadow your friendships. Keep sharing. Keep listening. Your friend will want to hear about and share your happiness, but what's going on in *her* life is important, too. Time spent talking, listening, and just being with this friend will only *add* to your happiness.

If you're feeling jealous of or competitive with a friend:

You're normal. As much as you might wish a friend well, it's not always possible to prevent feelings of competitiveness and jealousy.

Maybe, like Tom, you're trying to keep competitiveness over grades from spoiling a friendship.

Maybe the guy you've secretly liked for a long time has just asked your friend to go with him (and only *you* know that your heart is breaking!).

Maybe you have a friend whose life is exactly the way you'd like yours to be. Maybe he or she is great looking or really outgoing or seems to make top grades without studying much or has just made the cheerleading squad—and you didn't.

How can you be jealous—and still be a good friend?

For a start, admit to yourself that you're feeling jealous—and why. (Admitting these feelings to yourself—and realizing that this is *your* problem, not his or hers—will keep you from doing or saying hurtful things to your friend, like minimizing her good news or finding fault with him or her unfairly just to keep from having to talk about the good things that are happening to her.)

Knowing why you're jealous can give you some clues about what you feel you lack, what you might want to change in your life, if that is possible.

If you're jealous because your friend did better than you did on a class project, you might ask yourself: "How can I do my very best next time? How can I improve my *own* performance?" Keep the emphasis on your own abilities and performance. What's important is that you do *your* best. Maybe, in doing so, you'll make the top grade next time. Or maybe you won't. But when you know you did the very best you could do, you're not as likely to resent your friend.

If your secret love has yet to notice you're alive, but has asked your friend out, your heartbreak is understandable. Assuming that your friend didn't know about your feelings or that she isn't the kind of person who tries to get asked out by a guy the minute you tell her you like him (in which case, she may not be a real friend), you need to let your grief and disappointment happen privately and then go on with the friendship. You will love again, and maybe the next time you'll feel enough confidence to show that you like him or help him to notice you in a special way. It's true that no relationship can truly replace another. And it doesn't mean that you won't hurt a lot right now—or that you won't feel pretty jealous of your friend for a while. But you will survive. And a good friendship can weather this crisis, if you can look beyond your pain to all the good things you and she share together.

Maybe you need to change a certain attitude in your own life. If winning and being on top is the only way you can feel good about yourself, you're in a pretty precarious position. We all have disappointments—and can learn as much from mistakes and failures as we can from our successes. You are an important, special person whatever your grade point average, your test scores, your class rank, or whether or not you made the cheerleading squad or the basketball team. If you're male and feel threatened because a female friend is achieving more than you are in some area, give yourself a break! Would you feel the same way if a male friend got a better grade? Times are changing and you don't *have* to be better in all ways than your female friends. You *can't* be better in all ways. This doesn't mean that you're not completely masculine, that you're not a success. It simply means that this friend, like all your other friends, has certain special talents, and some of these may exceed yours. But you can learn a lot from and really enjoy each other!

If you're jealous of a friend over something that really can't be changed, maybe your expectations of yourself are unrealistic. Maybe your friend has talents and strengths that you don't have. In the same way, you have special gifts and abilities that he or she doesn't have. That's why friendships enrich our lives so much. We each bring something unique to our relationships.

If you find yourself envying a friend's sense of style or ease with people, tell him or her that you wish you could look as fashionable or meet people as easily as he or she does. Ask for help. Letting your friend know what you both appreciate and envy and asking for help can bring you even closer.

If you've had a fight with a friend:

Stop waiting for an apology or the assurance that you were right after all. Be the first to call a truce. Even if you're convinced that your friend was wrong, show your caring by saying, "I'm sorry that this has come between us. Our friendship is more important to me than any argument or misunderstanding. I've missed you. And I'm sorry we quarreled."

Some years ago, the popular movie *Love Story* was advertised with the slogan: "Love means never having to say you're sorry." That's just not true! Being close to another may mean caring enough to say "I'm sorry" many, many times—and forgiving many more times.

Being able to put your friendship ahead of your differences, your irritations, your rivalries, and your mistakes with each other is a sign of true caring, a sign that your friendship was meant to be and will bring you joy for a long time to come.

HOW TO KEEP FRIENDS (AND WHAT TO DO WHEN A FRIENDSHIP FADES)

Can you help me? I make lots of friends, but they never last very long! Pretty soon things go wrong and that person doesn't like me any more. Or I lose interest for a while and then the person thinks I hate him or her. What can I do?

Melissa T.

I'm crying my eyes out. My best friend is moving away, like 2,000 miles away! I can't stand to lose her as a friend! She says we can still be friends, but I'm scared she'll find a new best friend at her new school and forget about me.

Hilary J.

I just turned 14 and have this friend Mark who is 16. We live next door to each other and have always hung around together. Because he's two years older, he has always treated me sort of like a kid, which is getting to be a problem now that I'm getting older. He doesn't act like he likes me as much now that I'm more mature, too. What can I do?

Travis K.

Some friendships can survive for years—for a lifetime—and separations of many miles. Other friendships fizzle in days or weeks or after the first argument.

What makes the difference between a friendship that lasts and one that doesn't?

Friendships that don't last are often hastily made and end when the people involved realize that they don't have much in common. Some are based on inequality—like the relationship that Travis has had with his older friend—and fade when the younger person begins to grow up and wants a more equal friendship. And some friendships die of neglect. This can happen whether you're 2,000 miles apart or sitting next to each other in class. If you go through periods of ignoring each other, not keeping in touch emotionally, not giving as much as you're getting, your friendship can wither.

What can you do if your friendship is in trouble and you want to save it? Try talking with your friend. Travis might tell Mark how much he enjoys their friendship, but now that he's older, he doesn't like being treated like a little kid. He might say, in his own way, "Let's find a new way to be friends." Even if things don't work out (some people *prefer* unequal friendships), Travis will know that he tried.

What if you and your best friend are facing a move that will put you in different schools or so far apart that it will be difficult to visit often?

Your friendship can stay strong—if you and your friend want it that way. Long-distance friendships take extra care, but can be well worth the effort. Write letters. Make these like a visit by writing exactly the way you would talk to your friend if he or she were beside you. Make a cassette tape if writing still feels too impersonal. Talk on the phone from time to time as a special treat. Remember each other's special occasions: birthdays, significant events (for example, call your friend the day you know she's getting her braces off). Share your changes: Send pictures, let him or her know your real feelings—as if you were physically together. It's possible that, as you change, you will grow apart. But it's possible, too, that as you and your friend share your changes and discoveries over the years, you will become closer than ever.

Even friendships that don't last are important in our lives. We learn from our friends. We grow as the result of being close to others. And we give a lot to others through friendships, maybe more than we can ever know. The ability to love and share with others is something that you carry with you for a lifetime.

And some friendships *do* last a lifetime. These long-term relationships aren't perfect. They will weather some down times and some happy times, some times when you feel especially close and other times when you don't hear from each other for a while. But, in your hearts, you know you're there for each other. You will share a lot of joy and a lot of pain. You will need to work hard to keep up with each other's changes and the different directions your lives may be taking. But this kind of friendship is well worth the work and the effort. It is a special, gentle form of love that can enrich your life today and always.

CHAPTER FIVE

How to Cope with (or Avoid) Total Embarrassment

I'm 13 and everything is embarrassing. My parents embarrass me all the time. People laugh at my clothes because my family can't afford to get the brand-name ones that are in at my school. I wear a D-cup bra and boys tease me and call me things like "Lumpy Leslie." I embarrass myself, too. It seems like I spill something in the cafeteria every day or trip or say something really dumb when this boy I really like is around. Some days I hate to get up and go to school!

Leslie L.

This is a time of life when embarrassment is at an all-time high. It's a time when you're self-conscious about your changing body. It's a time when you may be unsure of yourself socially and very sensitive to criticism or teasing from others about your body, your clothes, or your behavior. It's a time when you're trying to separate from your parents, trying to be your own person, and part of this process can be finding fault with your parents and feeling embarrassed both by them or being seen with them by classmates or friends (who, you fear, might think you're a baby for doing things with your parents).

In short, during the early teen years, opportunities for total embarrassment abound.

But some embarrassments rank especially high. What *are* some of these—and what can you do about them?

MY BODY IS EMBARRASSING!

I can't convince my mom to let me get a bra. I am totally flat, but I'm 12 and everyone else in my class wears a bra. It's bad enough to be as skinny and flat as an eight-year-old, but what's even worse is wearing this stupid undershirt that everyone laughs at when I have to change for gym!

Sara J.

93

I'm overweight. I ought to lose about 20 pounds but I can't stick to a diet. What's really embarrassing is when my friends want to go to the beach and I say "No" because I don't want anyone to see me in a swimsuit. My thighs are just gross! But my friends think I don't want to be with them, and I'm too embarrassed to tell them it's because I'm fat.

Janet M.

I'm short for my age and still look like a kid. What's embarrassing is when I go to school dances and none of the girls want to dance with me because they're taller. What can I do?

Rob A.

I swear to God I'm the only person who sweats, I mean, really sweats in my whole school! My hands are cold and sweaty. I always have big wet rings under my arms that are so embarrassing! Nobody else has this problem. I keep my jacket on most of the time now so no one can see, and I'd be embarrassed to hold hands with anyone. How can I stop sweating so much?

"Sweat City"

Body changes (or lack of body changes) can be a special source of embarrassment right now. Never have you had such a need to look like your friends—and never will you all look so different from each other. Why? Because each person has his or her own internal timeclock for physical development.

Some people start developing as early as the ages of eight or nine. For girls who start getting breasts, and who gain the normal weight that gives womanly curves to the body and start menstruating while still in grade school, these changes can be especially embarrassing because they make one look and sometimes feel so different from friends. Studies show that boys who start developing early suffer less because being taller and looking more mature than classmates is often seen as an advantage for a boy.

But whether you're male or female, looking different from most of your friends *can* be embarrassing when you really don't want to stand out from the crowd.

What can you do if your body is embarrassing you?

Realize That You're Normal. This won't take away your embarrassment completely, but it can be reassuring. "Normal" has a very wide range, not only during these growing years, when people grow and develop at very different rates, but also later on. Have you ever looked—really looked—at a crowd of people and noticed all the different shapes and sizes? Normal people come in all sizes.

Sometimes what is embarrassing you will change. You will develop eventually. You will grow. If you're an early bloomer, the other kids will start catching up with you soon.

But sometimes you're faced with something that won't change. Maybe you'll *always* be shorter or taller than the average person. Maybe, because your body shape is naturally rounded, you'll never be model-skinny. Maybe you have a quite visible disability. You're still normal. It's normal for you to be short or tall or round. And your disability is a part of you, but not *the* most important part of you. You're still like everyone else in so many ways.

Accepting your body as both unique and normal can help you to start getting past your embarrassment.

Change What Can Be Changed—If You Want To. If you're embarrassed about excess weight, check with your doctor to get his or her recommendations about how much you can safely lose, and ask for some dietary suggestions. Get active. Actually, exercise can be a wonderful way to get rid of excess weight without starving yourself in the process.

If you're skinny and self-conscious, check again with your physician to see if your weight is normal for your age and height, and get his or her recommendations if you're underweight. Weight training can help to build shapely muscles in both males and females. And dance training can give you a good shape, too.

If you have leg hair that your parents won't let you shave yet, try bleaching to make the hair less obvious. Or ask your parents if a hair removal creme would be all right.

If you're embarrassed about perspiration, try a number of anti-perspirant/deodorants until you find one that works for you. (The ones containing the ingredient *aluminum chlorohydrate* as the major ingredient are most effective.) Shower or bathe daily. If that still doesn't work, think about what you're wearing. If you wear a lot of nylon, polyester, or other synthetic fabrics that don't "breathe," this could be part of the problem. Switch to clothes made of cotton and other natural fabrics. This can make a real difference. And don't wear a sweater or jacket all the time to hide perspiration. It will just make it worse.

It's also important to remember that perspiration is normal. Everyone does it. But, during the early teenage years, as the sweat glands are developing fully, they may work overtime. It won't always be this way. In the meantime, be aware that stress, nervousness and, yes, embarrassment, too, can make you sweat even more. So try to relax as much as you can in stressful situations. Pause. Close your eyes. Breathe deeply. Tell yourself that you'll be fine. Socially, get into the conversation, listen, concentrate on having a good time, and try to forget, as much as possible, about perspiration or sweaty hands. You may find that the less you worry about perspiration, the less you'll perspire!

If you're embarrassed because you don't have a bra, talk with your mother again. You may not need a bra physically, but getting one so that you'll feel less different from your friends can be important psychologically. That's what "trainer bras" are for. It's fine to be an individual and, if wearing undershirts or no bra doesn't bother you, there's no reason to change. But if you're embarrassed and upset by your lack of development—and your different underwear just makes this worse—there's no harm at all in a trainer bra to help you feel, for now, more like everyone else.

Compensate for Differences That Embarrass You. Body differences that are embarrassing to you now may change in time or you can change them over a period of time. But these aren't likely to change overnight. And, of course, there are some ways you may always be a little different, some things that really *can't* be changed.

The secret to overcoming your embarrassment in any of these instances is in developing skills or a winning attitude that can help you (and others) forget about your embarrassment or your differences.

Developing a warm, sensitive personality and a sense of humor can make up for a lot. If, for example, you're a short guy, having a good personality, a winning way with people, and excellent dancing skills (take cotillion or other classes or rent a dance-instruction video and practice with a friend or relative) may make you popular with girls anyway.

Pursue interests, hobbies, and causes you believe in. When you're involved and excited by life, being short or tall or thin or overweight or having a physical disability will become much less important or embarrassing to you or obvious to others.

ADULTS ARE EMBARRASSING ME!

My parents insist on us doing things "as a family" on weekends. It's SO embarrassing to have to go to the mall with my MOM (and all my friends see us there)! Not to mention going to movies with my parents who get really bent out of shape if I don't want to sit with them. They act like I was two years old!!

Shelley Z.

I have this teacher who embarrasses me by reading all my essays as examples to the class. It's just awful because everyone thinks I'm stuck up and teacher's pet. I tried to talk to my parents about this, but they just said I should be proud that my teacher thinks my work is so good. But I'm not proud! I'm embarrassed! What can I do?

Lisa K.

I have this problem. What do you do about your parents' friends who try to make conversation with you by saying things like, "Oh, you're really growing," or, "Last time I saw you you were a little kid!" or, "How's school?" I mean, how do you even reply to stuff like this? I just stand there beet-red and feel embarrassed for them and for me.

Joel W.

Help! I'm about to be totally embarrassed on what should be a really happy day: my eighth grade graduation! The problem is, my grandmother is coming over 1,000 miles to go to it and she dresses weird. She wears HATS! Nobody wears hats!! I just know she'll wear one and then everyone will make fun of me and hate me. What can I do?

Bonnie B.

Adults, with all the best intentions, can embarrass you beyond belief.

Parents can be embarrassing just because they're there when you don't want them to be—because you may feel that doing things with your parents makes you look like a little kid. And other adults can be embarrassing when they single you out or try to make conversation or insist on hanging around you while looking or acting outrageous.

What can you do?

Look for Embarrassment-Reducing Compromises. You can't always have everything your way. Maybe your parents really like spending time with you. Maybe they are anxious not to lose touch with you now that you're growing up. Maybe your teacher likes to use student work as an example of excellence to inspire other students. But you may be able to change these embarrassing situations a little.

You might talk with your parents and work things out so that you can spend time with them *and* with your friends. Maybe you can schedule family activities in places and at times when you're not likely to run into your friends. Maybe you can go to the movies with your parents and sit with your friends, then have a snack with your parents afterwards to talk about the evening. Maybe you can schedule every other Saturday—or one day a month—to go to the mall or out to lunch with your mom, and make mall excursions on other days with your friends.

Keep in mind that your embarrassment about being seen with your parents is part of your trying to grow up and be a separate person. Other people really don't see you as a baby if you're with your parents at times. Even other people your age, especially those whose parents *don't* take time for them or can't be with them much, may think you're lucky to have parents who do want to spend time with you. (Remember that *other* people's parents rarely look as embarrassing as your own because you're not trying to look separate from them.) And if friends tease you about being with your parents, keep in mind that this teasing can be based on their own insecurity. They're scared of looking like babies, too, and may feel temporarily more mature when they can give you a hard time.

But if you can find ways to compromise—to spend some time with your family and some time with friends—you can have the best of both worlds!

With teachers who embarrass you by making you or your work an example to others, you might try a private, respectful talk. You might ask the teacher not to use you as an example as much or not to mention your name when he or she reads an essay. Anonymous student essays can also be inspiring to others. Many times adults forget that, in these sensitive years, being singled out for praise can be as embarrassing as being singled out in less positive ways. Ask your teacher to make comments to you in writing on the paper or in private. Tell him or her how much this praise means to you personally, but let the teacher know that it's very hard for you to deal with your classmates when they're feeling angry, left out, or just scornful because you seem to be favored. Your teacher may give you a break here—and may also have some coping suggestions for you.

Give People Credit for Trying—and Give Yourself a Break. When an adult starts an awkward conversation with you, that person is probably at least as embarrassed and uncomfortable as you are, and he is trying in the best way he can to be nice. In the same way, you don't have to make brilliant conversation. Just be nice until you're rescued by a parent or circumstances.

Adults tend to focus on your growth because it really is amazing to them. What has been very gradual for you (maybe too gradual) seems sudden to them. And that's all they can think about when they first see you. They aren't trying to be rude or too personal. They're just surprised and amazed. You can ease both your embarrassment by simply smiling and agreeing—and, if you can, by changing the subject. You might say something like, "Yes, you're right! I think I'm outgrowing my clothes faster than my parents would like. And I'm getting big enough now to be almost a challenge to my dad at tennis." (Or mention some other sport that you know the other person might be interested in—for example, "And I'm thinking of going out for football," or, "I'm getting interested in basketball.") If a person asks you how school is, just say fine and tell a humorous story about something that happened (if you have any) or smile and say something like, "Oh, just struggling along. You know how it is. But I'm really getting interested in . . . . debate (or drama or the school paper or French club or sports)." These are cues for the conversation to switch to sports or some other area of mutual interest.

Face the fact that these conversations are never likely to be that great or that long. If the person is a visitor to your home and you've reached the end of your conversational rope and are working up to total embarrassment, make sure the person is comfortably seated, offer to get him or her something to drink or a snack, show him or her something that might be of interest, or excuse yourself to call your parent—or to let your parent and the friend talk privately.

Realize That You Are a Separate Person and Are Not Truly Responsible for a Relative Who Acts Or Dresses Outrageously. Fine. Great. But what if this person who wears funny hats or has this incredible laugh is about to invade your school territory for graduation or a school play or some other gathering where all your friends will be there to see?

First, remember that your relative may look or seem much more outrageous to you than to others. People notice different things about others, and your friends may see your relative in quite a different way than you do.

I'll never forget the time my beloved Aunt Molly came almost 3,000 miles to attend my eighth grade graduation. She had a habit, back then, of dressing in loud colors and wearing huge hats. As a family, we used to joke about Molly's wild outfits. But when she showed up at my graduation with this humongous hat with larger-than-life red roses all over the top of it, I nearly died of embarrassment! I waited for my classmates to find me and say, "Are you related to that lady in the silly hat?"

But no one seemed to notice or be embarrassed by the hat. People at graduation noticed Molly because she was fun to talk with, had a laugh that made others want to laugh along with her, and because she was (and is) a fascinating person. My teachers and classmates—the ones who weren't so preoccupied with their own families that they didn't even notice her (and there were a lot of those)—wanted to meet this special person I had always talked about so much. And I started to think about how much she must love me to come all that way to my graduation, and how proud I was of her as a person.

The more I thought about it, the more I realized that, even if other people *had* made fun of her hat, it wouldn't have mattered for long. And even if she hadn't been so interesting to others, she was still special to me. What mattered most was that this very special person was there for *me*—for my graduation.

If you have a relative who is likely to overdress for a school occasion, it might help if you ask another adult to let this person know discreetly that people will be dressing more casually or that the dress of the evening will be definitely low-key. If the adults in question have a sense of humor, the one doing the informing might even say, "We're supposed to be invisible and not embarrass anyone. You know how embarrassing we can be at this age!"

And even if you have a relative who is hopelessly outrageous, remind yourself that you *are* separate. You are *not* responsible for this person, which can be a comfort if he or she is pretty bizarre. If people laugh or tease you about this relative, don't let them see your embarrassment. If you can shrug and say something like, "What can I tell you? That's just the way she is! She's her own outrageous person," you'll be less likely to be teased. And you may be pleasantly surprised when others find this person's unusual dress or behavior charming or fun or interesting. You may be able to see this relative in a new and more positive way—through the eyes of your friends!

MY FRIENDS ARE EMBARRASSING ME AND I'M EMBARRASSING ME!

I have this friend who's fine as long as there are no girls around. If there are girls around, he acts like a real jerk, making all kinds of noises and comments that make them disgusted. What's worse is that they just assume we're BOTH jerks. I like my friend, but I think he's killing my social life.

Ted S.

There is this girl I like but people make fun of her because she doesn't have good clothes. Her family can't afford brand-name stuff, and people tease her about that. I'm afraid they'll start to hate me because I hang around with her, but I like her a lot.

Juliane P.

I get embarrassed when I'm around a boy I really like and I can't think of anything to say, or I start giggling and turning red and he thinks I'm some kind of space cadet. How can I look more mature to guys and stop embarrassing myself?

Donelle J.

Help! I got up in class yesterday and while I was giving my answer, I said a word wrong and everyone laughed. It was so embarrassing! I just stood there like a nerd. I got all red and felt like crying. Everyone laughed at me—even the teacher. What scares me is that no one will ever forget about this and I'll get teased for the rest of my life!

Priscilla W.

What can you do when being around a friend means risking embarrassment yourself?

• Help your friend to act in more appropriate ways. If you have a friend who is pretty normal most of the time but horribly embarrassing around the opposite sex, it is an act of kindness to help this person find a more appropriate way to be around others. It's not unusual for guys in junior high, some of whom may feel pretty ill at ease around girls, to try to get their attention by making strange noises, rude remarks, teasing, or grabbing (and going through) their purses.

If you can convince your friend that loud belches, comments about breast size, and purse raids are not the way to a girl's heart, you'll be doing him a big favor. (If you can convince your girlfriend that calling a guy ten times a night and hanging up when he answers, or writing this guy she hardly knows love notes in class and passing these along for everyone to see (and the teacher to confiscate), or sending squadrons of friends to ask him 900 times a day if he likes her is not likely to make his heart grow fonder, you'll be doing *both* of them a favor!)

If your friend is being made fun of because of poor grooming habits, be a real friend and help him or her to improve these. Offer hairstyling or make-up advice or share something in a magazine you found helpful yourself. If your friend has a problem with body odor, tell him or her in a nonhurtful way and offer some helpful suggestions. This is so personal that he or she may be really embarrassed at first, but, in most cases, will be glad you said something.

If your friend has no fashion sense—and is suffering because of this—offer to help her co-ordinate her outfits or let him know that, unless he really likes clashing plaids and is looking to make his own fashion statement, it might be better to wear a plaid shirt with solid-color pants.

However, if your friend has no problems with the way he or she dresses, see this embarrassment as *your* problem. The best way to deal with this may be to tell yourself that every person has his own taste and, as long as your friend is happy, that's what is most important. Your tastes don't have to match for you to be friends. You're separate people. And other people who don't realize that simply may not be as mature as you are right now.

• Realize that there are all kinds of embarrassing behavior. And people who make fun of other people because they don't have or can't afford expensive brand-name clothes are the most embarrassing of all. Ultimately, these self-appointed fashion critics are showing their shallow values and mean-spiritedness by teasing others about their less expensive or less trendy clothes.

How can you help a friend (or yourself) deal with their jeers?

If you really *want* the brand-name clothes because *you* like them (or your friend likes them), think of less expensive ways to get them. Brand-name merchandise is often available for very little money in thrift stores, at swap meets, and via garage sales. If you're patient, you can also find it marked down at regular department store sales. And if the family budget will not stretch to accommodate high-priced fashions, think of ways you might earn money—with baby-sitting or a paper route—to be able to afford some of the things you want. But what's important is that *you* like and want these things. It doesn't make sense to spend your money on something you privately think is silly or unattractive, but that everyone is wearing.

And if the money just isn't there in any way for you or for your friend, life does go on. The fashion trend will change again and again. And it's never too early to develop your own sense of style and flair. Sometimes, making your *own* fashion statement can get you positive attention.

For example, one mother helped her teen daughter to cope with fashion peer pressure by buying a pair of well-made but non-brand-name jeans and then embroidering the family name *backwards* on the back pocket. The family name (Spragle) came out "Elgarps." As it turned out, everyone wanted to know where she got these terrific mystery jeans, everyone wanted "Elgarps." The mother reports, "My girls still laughingly refer to the Elgarps theory when things are priced out of range."

Think about it. Who decides what is *in*? Maybe, with your originality, you (or your friend) could start a new fashion trend. And, if not, you or she may still grow in confidence by listening to your (her) own taste preferences instead of just following along. And if these taste preferences are expensive and out of line with budget reality, remember that there are *many* ways to be special and clothes are only one way. More important assets are being a caring friend, a kind and sensitive person, and having a good sense of humor.

What about when *you* embarrass yourself—all by yourself? Invariably, this happens around someone you really like and want to impress or in front of a big crowd.

Those two facts give you an important clue: You're most likely to embarrass yourself when you're feeling self-conscious and nervous to begin with.

So what can you do to avoid total embarrassment?

- Relax as much as you can . . . and act as if you weren't nervous. This isn't easy. But if you can do it, you'll be amazed at how much less embarrassment you'll have to face and how cool people will think you are.

For example, if you fall apart when you're around someone you really like, try convincing yourself that this person is just . . . another person. If boys in general make you crazy, act the way you would with a girlfriend and don't try to change your attitude or behavior. If you're tongue-tied around girls, pretend she's your sister or someone else you find nonthreatening. This pretending doesn't have to go on forever, just until you begin to feel comfortable enough with this person so you're not likely to embarrass yourself.

If speaking in front of the class (or, even worse, a school assembly) makes you want to crawl into a hole, try another mind trick or two. Focus on one person who looks friendly and supportive and direct your first few comments to him or her. Act as if everyone in the class (or the audience) was a close and loving friend. Or imagine that everyone listening to you is eating lunch (and half ignoring you) or dressed like clowns—or whatever makes them seem less threatening to you.

And remember that, when you mess up and people laugh, much of this laughter is relief (that they're not up there making that mistake) and most people's memories are fairly limited. You may remember your gaffe for a long time, but chances are, most people will forget pretty fast. People, especially in these vulnerable years, are so worried about themselves that they're not likely to dwell for long on something *you* did.

- When there's nothing else to be done—laugh! When people laugh over something you do or say, they don't always mean to be unkind. Maybe it really *was* funny. Especially if you make a mistake during a talk or speech, people relax and listen more carefully after they have laughed. Maybe they feel more warmth and connection with you.

I'll never forget the day, in ninth grade, when I had to introduce a special presentation at a school assembly. Feeling nervous and shy, I stepped up to the microphone, gazing out over the entire student body and faculty assembled in the auditorium. My heart pounded as I glanced at the first sentence on my notecard: "Today, we will be discussing . . ."

I cleared my throat and began, "Today, we will be *disgusting* . . ."

There was one moment of awful silence. I froze, hoping no one had noticed. No luck. A huge roar of laughter went up, filling the whole auditorium. Students laughed. Teachers laughed. Even the janitor, standing in the back, laughed. Finally, I laughed, too, and, acting as if this had just happened with a group of good friends (the thought of the real situation was just too horrifying), I continued, "Well, I hate to disappoint you, but this will actually be a tasteful *discussion* . . . ." We all laughed again and then I went on, actually feeling pretty good.

Because we *all* had a good laugh at the time, nobody teased me about my mistake, that day or ever. And I'm sure—well, pretty sure—that I'm the only one who remembers the incident today.

If there's a choice between laughing and crying—choose to laugh. You'll feel better, and so will everyone else. Laughter really does help chase away painful embarrassment!

You will always have some embarrassing times—all your life. But as you grow in self-confidence, as you become more and more your own separate, mature person, you won't be embarrassed as often or as easily as you may be now.

As you feel more at ease with yourself and others, you will find it easier to shrug and say, "Oh, well . . ." instead of "Oh, no!"

You will be less likely to fear embarrassment and more likely to face those embarrassing moments when they do happen, not with blushes or tears, but with wonderful, healing laughter.

CHAPTER SIX

Liking, Loving, Losing, Loving Again: All About You and the Opposite Sex

I'm 12 and in seventh grade. I have a big problem: All the boys in my class are so immature I can't stand them. They just act gross. Also, most of them are pretty short, and since I'm almost 5' 7", I'd feel funny going to a dance with one of them. There is this guy I like a lot who lives down the street. He's 16, has a car, and I think he likes me, but my parents have a fit and say I have to date someone my own age. But I hate the boys my own age! What can I do?

Deidre C.

What do girls want??? I'm 13 and I don't think I'm conceited when I say I'm nice and not ugly. I try to be polite and a good friend. Now I have plenty of friends, but no dates! The girls are always complaining about what beasts guys are, but they don't even look at someone who acts decent!

Roger S.

These early teen years are exciting and frustrating ones for boy-girl relationships. Discovering each other in a new way is exciting. But building a close relationship with another person can be frustrating with both of you going through so many changes and uncertainties, and when you're both not quite sure how to be with each other.

Girls in junior high tend to be physically and, quite often, emotionally more mature than their male classmates. Girls may tower over most boys at school dances. Girls may long for good conversations and romantic gestures when a lot of boys still think that making strange noises and pulling pranks is the way to a girl's fond attention—and to her heart.

Yet there can be problems when a girl in junior high tries to go out with a boy in high school. Her parents may object. She may not fit in with his more experienced and mature crowd of friends. He may have much more dating experience and expect more of her than she feels comfortable giving. (Levels of maturity vary, of course, but it's generally better, in these early years, to try dating guys your age or who are, at most, only a year or two older.)

Especially at the beginning of junior high, just being noticed by the opposite sex and finding a first real boyfriend or girlfriend is a special concern.

There are some who think that being liked or being loved or having someone special to go around with will simply *never* happen to them!

WHEN THERE'S NO SPECIAL LOVE IN YOUR LIFE

I'm so upset. I'm 13 and have never had a boyfriend. It isn't because I don't want to. I do! But boys don't notice me or like me. Everyone else is going out and having fun while I'm staying home watching TV on Saturdays and never having any fun at all. What can I do to get a boy to like me? I'm desperate!!!

Shaunna L.

What can you do if girls like you as a friend, but nothing more? It makes me feel bad when they tell me all their problems with the guys they're seeing, but nobody thinks of me that way.

Ryan J.

Do these feelings sound familiar?

Sometimes you can find yourself on the sidelines because of shyness. You may seem aloof and uninterested to others, and people are most attracted to others they feel are interested in them. No one is eager to risk rejection.

What can you do?

You can participate in school activities you enjoy. You'll have a chance to meet others in a more natural, relaxed way. And the people you meet will share some of your interests and beliefs, no small thing when it comes to building a good relationship with another person.

Show interest in someone: Smile and say "Hi." Ask a question or his/her opinion about something. Give the person you like a sincere compliment. Share your own opinion about something. Remember something important to that person: Wish him or her happy birthday, ask how a certain project turned out, or whether he/she plans to go out for a certain activity this year.

What if the person *still* hardly knows you're alive? What if you're pretty much ignored or even rejected by this person despite your show of interest?

Rejection is always a risk and it can be hard to take. You may never really know why the person acts this way. Maybe he or she is in a bad mood that has nothing to do with you. Maybe this person is dating someone else outside of your school, or recently broke up with someone and isn't ready to have another relationship just yet. Maybe the person likes a particular physical type—and you're not it! Maybe this person just doesn't like you for reasons even he doesn't understand.

Even though it's hurtful to you, this person's rejection of you, especially if he or she is cruel about it, is really a problem for him or her. Being cruel to another can signal deeper problems. Being unable to see the value of others past certain physical types may limit one's ability to have a really intimate relationship now or ever. And if a person fails to see your charms because of dating another or recovering from a breakup, that's *still* his or her problem—because this person is missing out on getting to know and like *you*!

Keep in mind that, whatever a particular boy or girl thinks, you're a very special person with a lot to offer. The best thing you can do is to keep growing as a person and value yourself whether or not you're dating at the moment. Other people don't make you special. Having a date—any date—every Saturday night doesn't make you special. YOU make you special. And there will be those who eventually see and appreciate the wonderful person you've grown to be.

What if people *do* appreciate you, but they tend to see you as a friend instead of in a romantic way?

Believe it or not, having close friendships with those of the opposite sex is an *excellent* way to prepare for good, loving relationships. You may end up better off than your classmates who simply jump into dating right away without getting to know much about those of the opposite sex. When you rush into romance, it's easy to get locked into roles and ways of behaving that might not lead to future happiness.

If, on the other hand, you develop close and caring friendships with those of the opposite sex, you will have a better understanding of their feelings and why they act the way they do.

Some of the very best romantic relationships grow from strong friendships. And even if current friendships never take a romantic twist, they can teach you a lot about how to be close and understanding with another person and prepare you well for falling and growing in love with someone special.

HOW TO BE ATTRACTIVE TO OTHERS

What can you do if you're not tall and not a jock type? Girls at my school all go for those guys even if they act horrible and treat them bad. How can a nice, but average-looking person get a girlfriend?

Jonathan M.

I'm not beautiful and because of this it's like I'm invisible to guys. How will I ever have a boyfriend when none of them know I'm even alive?

Sherri S.

It's quite common in the junior high years (when many people are feeling insecure about their own looks and their worth) for a lot of boys and girls to want to go out mostly with people whose physical beauty or status (or both) will tell the world, "Hey, this person must have something special to be going out with someone so obviously outstanding!"

Of course, this borrowed glory is often temporary and always insecure. And some of these relationships, which may have little to do with the real personalities, interests, and feelings of the people involved, may not be very satisfying in private.

And, if you're looking for a relationship that will bring you closeness and real acceptance for and from another person, it has to be based on a lot more than looks and status.

So how can you be more attractive to others when you're not handsome or gorgeous or a cheerleader or jock?

Like Yourself First. This doesn't mean being conceited. It means feeling good about the unique person you are. Good feelings about yourself—called good self-esteem—can give you an air of confidence that others find very attractive. If you like yourself, others will, too.

If, on the other hand, you drag around feeling horrible and desperate for a date, any date, people will be inclined to avoid you.

As you begin to feel and look more confident, others will be drawn to you. And these good feelings about yourself will help you to reach out and show interest in others (instead of worrying so much about yourself)—and that can make you practically irresistible!

Discover and Cultivate the Best Parts of Your Personality. Maybe being the life of the party, being witty and outgoing, just isn't *you*. But even if you're quiet, you can show your charm by listening, asking questions that encourage others to talk and share their feelings and opinions. You don't have to talk a lot to be considered a good conversationalist. You don't have to be super-outgoing to be considered a warm and caring person. You don't have to come up with all kinds of funny lines to have a good sense of humor. Seeing humor in everyday life, appreciating witty remarks others make, and being able to laugh at yourself are all wonderful, endearing personality traits!

Develop Your Own Interests and Your Own Point of View. If you're passionately interested in certain things, if you develop skills that make you feel good about yourself, if you're interested and involved in activities and causes, this can make you attractive to others.

How attracted would *you* be to someone who just sat around waiting for someone to come along to make life meaningful? Don't you find yourself drawn to people who are interested and interesting? Well, other people feel much the same way!

Besides, just sitting around and waiting for love to happen is really boring. You can have fun, enjoy your life, and grow in new and wonderful ways whether or not you're in love right now.

Take Good Care of Yourself. Good personal hygiene and grooming are a must! Being very handsome or beautiful is an accident of nature. But well-groomed good looks are available to anyone.

You don't have to have designer clothes. You don't have to be model-thin.

Find a hairstyle that looks right for you. Eat a healthy, well-balanced diet. Get regular exercise. Bathe or shower every day. Take good care of your hair, your nails, and your teeth. (This goes for guys, too. Dirty, ragged fingernails, greasy hair, and bad breath can be a turnoff for either sex.) If you're not clean and fit, even the most stylish, expensive clothes won't make you attractive.

If you're healthy, fit, clean and well-groomed, and your clothes are neat, clean and well-pressed, you'll look great—whatever your height or shape or facial features. Taking good care of yourself shows that you think you're *worth* it, and that sends a very positive message to others.

Be Kind and Sensitive to Others. There are all kinds of attractiveness—and perhaps the most important is being a good, caring person.

• Do you care about making others look and feel good and clever and attractive?

If you can help others in this way, you may find yourself worrying less about yourself and not being nearly so nervous.

• Do you give other people a chance to talk or do you monopolize conversations, trying to show how clever you are?

A good conversationalist is someone who can *share* feelings and opinions with others while encouraging them to share in the same way.

• Are you thoughtful? Do you remember birthdays or other special events? Do you give honest praise or comfort? Are you dependable?

People are attracted to thoughtful, dependable people. This can mean not taking your moods out on others, being on time instead of always late, keeping your promises to others, and respecting others' values and opinions—even when they're quite different from yours.

I go out a lot, but mostly with different people because I almost never get asked out more than once or twice by the same person. I'm really cute. Everyone says so. So what's wrong?

Bethany Q.

Dating around a lot isn't all that unusual in junior high. This is a time of discovering what kinds of people you like most, what kinds of dating and love relationships fit your needs best. It's quite rare to find lasting love that grows into a lifetime commitment at this stage of your life. It *can* happen, but it isn't common. This doesn't mean that you can't experience real love. It simply means that many people aren't ready to commit themselves to one person or settle into a long relationship at this stage of life.

But if you *never* get asked out a second or third time, you may be doing something to turn others off. What could this be? The following is a list of common turnoffs discovered through an informal survey of teens from 12 to 15. Do any of these look painfully familiar to you?

A sure turnoff is someone who:

• Is always bragging about what he or she has or does or how rich his or her family is.
• Lies about doing all kinds of things you *know* he or she hasn't done.
• Is always trying to change a date's personality, clothes, or interests—even on a first date!
• Is totally self-centered and doesn't even know other people's feelings exist.

- Is jealous and possessive—even after only one or two dates.
- Tells everyone *everything* about what happened on a date (and maybe some stuff that *didn't* happen just to spice up the story a little).
- Goes on and on about previous dates and how awful or wonderful they were, telling details you never wanted to hear.
- Tries to act cool all the time.
- Is convinced everything he or she says or feels is right or true and everything anyone else says or feels is wrong.
- Smells bad or wears dirty or embarrassingly weird clothes.
- Tries to be a phony sophisticate—for example, by smoking or drinking a lot, swearing every other word, or pretending to have done everything or seen everything before, so nothing is new or exciting.
- Tries to take over another's life, expecting that person to always put his or her needs and feelings second.
- Answers "I don't care" or "Whatever you want" whenever asked what he or she wants to do that evening—especially if this person later complains about the date's choices!
- Is rude to your friends and tries to make you not like them anymore.
- Tries to force you to do something you don't feel right about—and puts you down for saying "No."

A lot of people who fall into these turnoffs are trying very hard—too hard—to get others to like them. You don't have to tell your life history, brag, or present your family's financial statement to be interesting to another person. In fact, these turnoffs can make you look boring, arrogant, and self-centered.

Simply being yourself, trying to help the other person feel comfortable and liked, and letting yourself have a good time (instead of trying to be constantly cool and sophisticated) can all help you to make a new start socially.

PARENTS VS. YOUR LOVE LIFE

My parents think I'm too young to date, even though I'm 13 and all my friends go out. What can I do about this?

"A Prisoner"

This is a common question in the early teens. Much depends on what you mean by "date." Boy-girl dances are common during these years. Going out in mixed groups is also a common way to socialize with people of both sexes without some of the pressures of individual dating. "Seeing someone" can mean meeting at the movies or mall. If dating means having car dates alone with an older guy, your parents may have a point. A guy that much older may have experience and expectations that far exceed yours.

But what can you do if you really like and want to go out with someone, or if you're in grave danger of becoming a social hermit against your will?

Talk with your parents. Tell them what you're feeling and how much freedom you think you're ready to handle. Listen to their feelings and opinions. Then try to find a compromise all of you can live with for the time being. Maybe they'll let you go to school or church dances. Maybe you can go around with a group and see someone within that group informally, but not have any dates with just the two of you. Maybe your parents will agree that you can see this one person if you meet at a movie or mall or if a parent can drive you on the date and take him or her home.

As embarrassing as all this sounds, it may be the only choice you have, for now, between completely defying your parents' wishes (and risking their wrath and the possibility of spending half your youth being grounded) or being a total social hermit.

Defying or ignoring your parents' rules, screaming, crying, and complaining that everyone else is having fun while you're stuck with parents who treat you like a baby is not going to do anything for your case. Parents get tense when you say things like "But everyone else . . ." This tends to convince them that they're the only sane parents around and that there's no way they'll back down now.

If you can show your maturity and willingness to compromise by agreeing, for now, to limit dating to group activities, or have parents drive and pick up, or whatever the restrictions might be, your parents will be likely to give you more freedom in the near future. Try the compromise for several months. Follow the rules carefully. Then ask your parents to reconsider and, perhaps, give you permission to stay out a little later, see one person in particular, or whatever step toward independence you'd like to take.

If it's any consolation, some of the kids who have too much freedom too soon may end up with more hassles and problems than they're ready to deal with. Saying "My parents won't let me . . ." may make you feel like a baby at times, but at other times it can be a real relief. It can get you off the hook in awkward situations. Contrary to your fears, most of your friends won't think you're a baby. They might feel sorry for you that you have such strict parents. And there may be others who wish their parents cared enough to set limits. (Even though they're not likely to tell you this directly.)

My mother gets all bent out of shape when I call a boy. She doesn't think it's right. But everyone does it. They just didn't in her day. I think my boyfriend's mother feels sort of the same way because she sort of sighs when I call and says, "Just a minute," without sounding too happy about it. How can I convince them that what I'm doing is all right?
Denise D.

It's not unusual these days for a girl to make the first move in asking a guy out or expressing interest in him. It's true that calling a boy (versus sitting futilely and forlornly by the phone waiting for him to call) isn't exactly considered the bold, brash act it may have been in your mother's youth.

On the other hand, before you dismiss your mom's (or his mom's) lack of enthusiasm as old-fashioned and hopelessly middle-aged, think about some of your actions.

• Do you call a guy you like with something specific in mind—to ask him to go someplace with you—or do you just call to get and keep his attention at all hours of the evening?

- Are you polite to the person who answers, greeting them, identifying yourself, and asking for your friend—or do you treat his family like an answering machine?
- Are you thoughtful about when you call: not too late at night nor early in the morning or during mealtimes?
- Do you limit your conversation or do you go on and on, tying up your phone and his?
- Do you play games with the phone and with him: calling and then hanging up about 20 times a day, calling with silly excuses or just to giggle in his ear?
- Do you keep calling even if he has asked you not to call him during a certain time—or at all? (This may not mean he doesn't like you, just that his family is teasing him about getting calls from a girl or that his parents are getting steamed because your calls are starting to intrude on their lives too much.)

If you can answer "Yes" to any of the above, maybe the parental objections have some merit.

While it's fine, these days, to take the first step in showing a boy you like him, it *isn't* okay to make a nuisance of yourself . . . or a fool of yourself. Doing so can sabotage what might otherwise be a promising relationship.

My parents just hate this girl I'm seeing. They don't like the way she looks or acts, which is older than she is (14). They think we should break up. We don't want to. What can I do to convince them to leave us alone?

Josh H.

My dad is such a pain. He thinks every guy who looks at me is some sort of pervert. And he is so suspicious of guys I go out with that I hate for them to come in the house. He especially hates this guy I'm going out with now. He criticizes his hair, his clothes, his manners, and the fact that he isn't a good student. But Larry (my boyfriend) is a really good person and he loves me. How can I convince my dad to like him?

Cherylyn L.

Parents may take a dim view of the person you're seeing for any number of reasons.

Maybe they don't object to the person *per se,* but to your exclusive involvement with each other. If this seems to be the case, talk it over with them and find out why.

Are they afraid that this relationship is taking too much time and energy that could be spent on schoolwork, your own interests, activities, household chores, and family life? Look at your schedule closely. All of these things are important in your life. If you get your household chores done, keep your grades up, and make some effort to spend time just for yourself and time with your family, your parents may be less alarmed and more accepting of your boyfriend or girlfriend.

Are they afraid you're trying to grow up too fast? Before you ask for more freedom, show that you can also take more responsibility. If you are careful about keeping curfew rules, letting your parents know where you'll be and with whom, and generally earn their trust, their anxiety and suspicion may fade. When they see that you can go out and nothing terrible happens, that you seem to be handling yourself in a mature way, they may relax and even come to like your boyfriend or girlfriend.

Are they afraid that you're spending so much time with this one person, that you're missing out on time and closeness with others? Remember that friendships are important, too. Don't drop all your friends the minute you fall in love. Make time just to be with your friends and time to make new friends through special activities or volunteer work. To grow as an interesting person, you need all *kinds* of active, caring people in your life. You need to learn to give in friendship as well as in love. If your parents can see that you're not neglecting friends, that you're not devoting your entire daily life to one person, their objections may ease.

Maybe your parents are afraid that you're getting into a sexual relationship that could limit your options and maybe even threaten your health and your life. Before you dismiss this as incredibly dumb and melodramatic, think about it. Teenage pregnancy is the main reason girls drop out of school and a major factor in their subsequent, often lifelong, poverty. It can limit a boy's life options, too. And sexually transmitted diseases really can threaten your health, your future fertility and, in the case of AIDS, your life. These diseases happen to nice people. They're happening to young people. And too many young people think, "It couldn't possibly happen to me!" and don't protect themselves by choosing not to have sex or, at the very least, by using reliable birth control and practicing safe sex (like using condoms). Your parents may worry that if you get very close to someone, you may have sex before you're ready emotionally and without thinking of the consequences. Is there any basis for this fear in your case? Talk with your parents about your values. Think about their concerns and take these seriously. Reassure them that you will not let yourself be swept away or talked into sex too soon. They may feel somewhat reassured.

But what if your parents hate, really hate, the person you're seeing—not for any of the above reasons—but for his or her own qualities?

Again, try talking and listening. Find out what their objections are. You may disagree with these, but when you listen to them, they'll be more likely to listen to your opinions, too.

If your parents don't like a date for certain physical traits—hairstyle, dress or the like—listen with respect and then point out this person's good points. Suggest that they invite this person to dinner or to share some family activity so they can see some of these good traits for themselves. If your parents have just caught a glimpse of your love in passing, the only impression they could have would be superficial. Ask them for a chance and give them a chance to see this person as you do.

If they know this person well and *still* hate him or her, try to discover if there's any truth to their objections. Maybe they've noticed something you haven't. Maybe this person treats you in a hurtful way, but you're too in love to see. Maybe he or she has a background or values that are so different from yours that your parents know from experience that this relationship will be a difficult, painful one. Their criticisms usually come from caring so much about you that they react strongly—and maybe over-react—when they sense that you might be hurt or taken advantage of by another. Take their feelings as a warning and as a way to make very sure that you're *not* being used or abused in your relationship.

Maybe your parents *are* over-reacting. Or maybe what they value in a person is very different from what you value. The best way to deal with this is to be tolerant of your differences. Don't argue that your date is *perfect* and deny that he or she has any faults. Being able to see and acknowledge a person's faults and love him or her anyway is part of mature love. When your parents see your maturity, they may feel a little less alarmed.

If your parents *always* dislike your dates, it could be their problem. Maybe they're having trouble letting go. Maybe they've had unhappiness in their own lives and don't trust *anyone* of the opposite sex and are carrying these feelings over to your relationships.

But it could be *your* problem, too. Ask yourself if you're choosing your dates, at least in part, because they're *not* acceptable to your parents. This is a common way to rebel. But it really isn't a way to show how independent you are. You're still letting your parents' tastes determine your choices.

A truly mature person chooses dates and friends on the basis of his or her own tastes and preferences and for their own personal qualities. Some may be people your parents don't like much. And some may even be a hit with your parents. What's important is that these are people who are *positive* influences in your life. You help each other to grow in new ways, to become better people for having known and loved each other.

DATING DILEMMAS

My boyfriend is so jealous! If we're at a party and I even look at another guy, he gets mad. How can I convince him to be less jealous?

Erin H.

This girl I'm seeing is totally paranoid. If I talk to another girl, she thinks I don't like her anymore. I have a lot of friends who are girls, but she doesn't understand.

Greg I.

Jealousy can come from insecurity. If you're seeing someone who is jealous a lot, do everything you can to help him or her to feel more secure. Express your appreciation and love. When you're with others, make it very clear that you're together (instead of abandoning him or her). Explain which people are strictly friends. And act in ways that make this clear. If you claim to be a friend with a girl, treat her like you would any other good friend without flirting. This can help a lot.

Some people who need to feel desirable and sought after by others try to have it both ways by flirting with others and making a date jealous. This is an excellent way to destroy trust. This kind of game playing creates more problems than it solves— and hurts people in the process. If you want to be truly desirable and have a close, caring relationship with another, don't do this.

On the other hand, if you're seeing someone who is unreasonably jealous, don't let his or her insecurity rule your life. It's important to have friends and your own life. It's important to spend time apart to pursue your own interests, dreams, and goals. If you're with a person who can't tolerate any independence on your part, even after you've talked reasonably about it, this person may be too immature and insecure to have a close relationship right now. This may not be the right person for you.

If you find yourself squeezing the life out of your relationships by being jealous and possessive, ease up. Give the other person some breathing space. You can't hold a loving relationship together with threats and ultimatums. If you're to have a happy future together, you both have to be free to choose, to grow as individuals, and to have interesting lives apart as well as together. Do you really want to hang onto someone with guilt and tears and threats? Think about it: It's much more of a compliment when someone freely chooses to be with you.

I have a slight problem with my boyfriend. When we're alone together, he's really sensitive and loving. But the minute we're with his friends, he starts acting like Mr. Macho, and either ignores me or bosses me around. I hate it! What can I do?

Jana K.

Private times together usually *are* the most special times in a relationship. We usually are somewhat different with each other when others are around. Sometimes this is out of consideration for others. Think of the times when you felt disgusted or embarrassed or lonely when you were with a couple who had eyes only for each other, even in a crowd. People who hug and kiss a lot and exchange private jokes and sentiments in front of others are being inconsiderate and showing off. You can be very much together and give a sense of caring about each other while still being interested and involved with the people around you.

On the other hand, some people do a hurtful turnabout in front of their friends, ignoring, putting down, or trying to dominate a date. This often happens—especially with boys—because people are afraid of being teased for showing tenderness. Maybe they feel pressure from their friends to be macho or seem independent.

What can you do about this? Talk with each other. Tell your boyfriend how you feel when he acts like this. Maybe you can compromise. If you understand why he doesn't act as close and romantic in front of his friends, maybe he will agree to tone down the macho bossiness. Maybe you can limit the amount of time you spend together with his friends, allowing each other time apart to be with friends. You need to let him know how his behavior affects you. He may be so busy trying to avoid embarrassing teasing from his friends that he doesn't realize you're feeling hurt.

And it's important to keep in mind that private, loving words and actions mean the *most* when they're shared by the two of you alone. That way, you *know* that when he is tender and loving he is doing this for *you*, not for show.

My girlfriend upsets me when she tries to change everything about me. If she likes me so much, why does she want to change everything from my clothes and hair to my personality?

Steve Y.

Most of us want the very best for someone we love and we try to help them to grow and change in ways that are best for them.

But sometimes this gets turned around. We get so involved in trying to help another person improve that we lose sight of that person's feelings and preferences. It sounds like that's what's happening with Steve and his girlfriend.

If you've found yourself trying to change another person, stop and think. The only person you *really* have the power to change is yourself. You can only *suggest* changes to another, and that person has a perfect right to go along with or *not* go along with your suggestions. Instead of trying to suggest that this person do a complete physical and personality makeover, think of the most important and most beneficial changes this person might make in his or her life. Suggest them. Offer to help. And then let it go. Only the other person can decide whether or not to make these changes.

If someone is trying to change you, tell him or her how you feel. You might say something like, "I appreciate your concern. I know you care about me. But I prefer this . . . I want to change in this other way . . ." By bringing your feelings out in the open, you can keep resentment from building on both sides and make very clear where one person's right to suggest stops and your own freedom to choose begins.

When I was with my former boyfriend, I did something I'm really ashamed of and rumors got around. Now I'm dating someone I really like and he wants me to do this, too. Even though I care about him, I don't want to do it. I'm afraid he'll think I don't like him as much as I did my former boyfriend, which isn't true AT ALL! What can I do???

"Desperate"

Why do guys want to know everything about other people you've gone out with? My boyfriend asks me all these questions, but if I tell him the truth, he gets mad and if I don't tell him anything, he thinks I have something wild and sleazy to hide. Help!!

Emily A.

Ghosts of former relationships can haunt your present in hurtful ways.

Maybe you find yourself talking a lot about former relationships to further convince the person you're seeing now that others, too, have found you desirable and fun to be with. But this is a sign of insecurity, not success. The *best* way you can convince someone that you're a good partner is to be the best you can be *here and now*! What happened with someone else has little, if anything, to do with what the two of you share now.

Maybe your date is curious about what happened with others. This can be a sign of insecurity, too. He or she may really be asking, "How do I fit into your life? Am I the most special to you? Do you like me best?" If you can concentrate on showing that person that you care and that he or she is Number One with you, these questions may come up less and less.

Maybe, like "Desperate," you're the victim of rumors—either true or false. If it's a false rumor, say so. If it's true, level with the other person in a caring way. You might say something like, "I really feel bad about what happened with that other person. It was a mistake. I choose not to do it again, even though I really care about you. Doing this with another person wasn't a sign that he (she) meant more to me. I simply had to learn the hard way what's right for me and wrong for me right now. I hope you understand. I really care about you a lot!"

Keep in mind that there are *all* kinds of ways you can show that you care.

Sometimes the most loving relationships don't involve sex—for a long time or ever. You don't have to "prove" your love for another by violating your own values. You don't have to repeat past mistakes just to avoid hurting someone's feelings. When you feel good about yourself and the relationship, you'll be better able to be a loving, caring partner!

This is really embarrassing, but I'll ask it anyway: How do you know how to kiss? Please don't think I'm stupid! I need to know. The thing is, if you do something wrong, everyone knows it and you get made fun of. Like this girl Patti in my class. She's miserable because some guys told everyone that she kisses like an alligator, whatever that means. How can I keep that from happening to me? It isn't that I haven't kissed anyone before. I'm 14. But I'm going out for the first time next week with a guy I like a lot and I want to make sure I kiss the right way!

Diana M.

Diana has a lot of company, even though she doesn't realize it. A lot of people worry about doing everything just right on a date: from saying just the right things to kissing perfectly.

Why does something as natural as kissing cause so much worry? Well, first, we aren't born knowing how to do this. It's a natural behavior, but an acquired skill. It takes time to learn how to kiss without bumping noses or feeling self-conscious. And you're likely to be twice as worried if you think you're being judged.

How can you ease your anxiety?

- Don't rush into anything. You don't have to kiss on a first date or do anything else that makes you uncomfortable. Talk with each other. Get to know each other. The more comfortable you feel with a person, the less likely you are to feel anxious and judged when it comes to kissing.

- Realize that people criticize and tease because of their own insecurity. People who set themselves up to judge or make fun of others usually do this to look like the experts they're not and to keep others from judging them. If you can *both* relax and just have a good time together, you'll both feel more secure and less likely to criticize each other's kissing technique.

- Accept some awkwardness as natural. Think of how you felt when you were just getting to know *any* close friend. You may have been a little shy and nervous at first. Maybe you didn't always know what to say to each other. It's the same way with dates. You may go through a time of temporary uneasiness between the time you decide that you want to know this person better and the time you begin to feel truly at ease with each other. Don't expect everything to be perfect. Holding hands with someone you're getting to know can be exciting, even if your hands *are* a bit sweaty. You don't have to kiss like a movie star in a passionate love scene to show affection. A short, simple kiss, especially if that's what feels most comfortable right now, can be as exciting as a long, passionate one. Bumping noses or feeling a little shy doesn't have to be a disaster. It's all part of learning and growing.

- Be selective. Avoid getting involved with people who kiss and tell and tease. Protect your tender feelings by going out with people you like and trust. Then when awkward moments happen, you'll feel free to laugh or reassure each other without fearing public ridicule or rejection.

What do you do when you want something different? My boyfriend thinks we should see other people. I don't want to see anyone but him. How can I convince him that we belong together?

"Heartbroken"

I'm scared that my boyfriend is going to drop me because I won't have sex with him. He has had sex before and wants to with me, but I don't feel ready. Yet, I'm scared of losing him. What should I do?

Tessa L.

Differences can be sad and scary.

If you've talked and argued and talked some more and you still can't agree, you need to focus on your own feelings and values.

What feels right for you right now?

If you want an exclusive relationship and the other person doesn't, try to look realistically at your situation. It may be that the other person just isn't ready for an exclusive commitment. Can you stay in a relationship knowing that he or she is seeing others? If the answer is "Yes," you need to cope with your disappointment over your differences and enjoy what you do share together. If the answer is "No," it may be time to call it quits—as heartbreaking as that can be—and find new ways to nurture yourself and, perhaps, find another person to love who *can* give you what you want and need.

Keep in mind that some people say, "I think we should see others," as a gentle way to begin a breakup. Could this be the case in your relationship? It takes two to make a relationship. If one person really doesn't want to be there, hanging on and trying to work things out doesn't make sense. Looking at things realistically is hard . . . when you wish so much that he or she would stay. But facing the fact that this relationship was not meant to last, facing all your sad and angry feelings, and then going on with your life can be much better for you than trying desperately to deny your differences and make a relationship work when it *can't* possibly work.

What if your differences are sexual?

Again, it makes sense to pay attention to your own feelings and values. It's very hard to say "No" to someone you care about, but if your relationship is meant to last, it will survive such differences.

Remember that having sex, especially if you feel pressured or forced, is not good for you or your relationship. Sex does not give you any guarantees that you'll be together forever. (If that were so, Tessa's boyfriend would still be with the first person he had sex with!) It doesn't create love where none existed before.

Losing a relationship is always a risk—whether or not you agree, whether or not you compromise your values. So it makes sense to listen to your own feelings first. You *can* differ with someone you love, you *can* say "No," and still keep your love and respect for each other. If your love for each other is real, you can accept each other's differences and enjoy the feelings and values you *do* share.

HOW TO TELL IF IT'S REALLY LOVE

My parents say it isn't possible to feel real love when you're my age (13), but I think it is. I love my boyfriend so much that I can hardly eat or sleep or concentrate in school for thinking of him! We can't stand to be apart. If this isn't love, what is it??

Samantha J.

I think I'm in love because I think my girlfriend is perfect! My mom says that's not love at all, but infatuation. What's the difference between real love and infatuation? How can I convince my mom that what I'm feeling is real?

Brad C.

Your feelings are real—whatever they happen to be.

Some people claim that, because you're young, you can't possibly be in love. That isn't true. You can fall in love at any age. Sometimes this love is immature and is called infatuation. Sometimes this love is mature and is considered the ideal way to love another person.

There's no age limit on either type of love. Immature love or infatuation is love that is limited by emotional immaturity or lack of experience. It can happen to people of all ages, not just young teens.

And mature love can happen at any age, too. What it means is that you're able to truly share with another.

How can you tell the difference between mature and immature love?

If your love is immature:

- Your main focus is on you. You're in love with the idea of being in love.
- You're jealous, possessive and clinging, and more concerned with what you can get than with what you can give to another.
- You think your partner is perfect. And the moment he or she shows any imperfection, you lose interest and maybe feel cheated and disillusioned.
- You are so distracted by your feelings of love and your relationship that you can't concentrate on other important areas of your life like eating, sleeping, studying, or spending time with friends.
- Your main attraction to the other person is based on his or her looks or status.
- You're convinced that this person can make you completely happy.
- You agree with each other, even when you disagree inside, because an argument might end the relationship.
- You fall in love fast and out of love fast. You have an urgent need to make a good impression and to promise each other anything.
- You feel that friends are friends—and less important—and romantic partners can't really be friends. You work on creating an aura of mystery and romance, and rarely, if ever, act like yourself in the relationship.

If your love is mature:

- You're in love with a *person* and his or her happiness is high on your priority list.

- You can enjoy being together and apart. There is time in your life for everything that's important—and being in love gives you *more* energy to do all the things you need to do.
- You accept each other's faults and differences. You can be human with each other. You encourage your partner to grow and change in ways he or she chooses.
- Physical attraction may be present, but it isn't the most important aspect of your love. You can also enjoy just being together and all the qualities in each other that make you special individuals.
- You know that you make your own happiness and fulfillment. You don't hold your partner responsible for that, but you *do* take pleasure in sharing your individual happiness with each other. And you know that, even if your relationship should end, you could survive and, in time, feel happiness again.
- You feel you have plenty of time to get to know each other. You don't feel any need to rush into actions or commitments that you're not ready for.
- You're not threatened by anger or temporary distance. You know that there are times of special closeness and times of pain in all love relationships. You accept your times of pain with compassion and trust and do everything you can to help each other . . . or to understand and support the other person when there's nothing else you can do for him or her right now.
- You are, first and foremost, loving, caring friends!

HOW TO SURVIVE A BREAKUP

How do you break up with a person without hurting their feelings? I don't want a big scene. I just want to break up. I was thinking of just not saying anything and just going out with another person. Is that better than going up to this girl and saying, "It's all over!"?

Shawn A.

I wrote my boyfriend a letter to say I wanted to break up and he's REALLY mad because I didn't tell him in person, and also because I told two of my friends before I told him. Is he being too sensitive?

Cissy T.

I'm crying my eyes out because my boyfriend broke up with me. I can't stand it when I hear our songs on the radio or when I see him at school sitting with someone else at lunch. I feel like my life is ruined because of this and I'll never love anyone as much again. What can I do to get him back?

Jennifer Z.

Breaking up is never easy—whether you're the one leaving or the one left.

If you want to break up with someone, don't just disappear or send word through your friends or the school rumor line. That's embarrassing and cruel. Letters are usually a bit too impersonal, but are okay if you're separated by considerable distance *or* you find it impossible to talk with each other. Usually, telling the person gently, directly, and *in private* is best.

Of course, you could say nasty things, embarrass the other person to death and leave little doubt that you think this person is a total jerk. But that's a bad idea for two reasons. First, you will add more hurt to an already hurtful experience for this person. Second, you'll feel bad about yourself because you've been deliberately mean. No matter how angry you feel at the moment, take a gentle tone with the breakup. You might say something like, "I just feel I'm not the right person for you. I feel we need to try other relationships." By keeping the emphasis on *your* feelings instead of his or her shortcomings, you can ease the other's pain a little.

If you're being left and you know, deep down, that the situation is hopeless, don't threaten, cry, and beg. You may buy a little more time, but the other person won't *really* be there for you emotionally.

So what can you do when there's nothing to be done?

Accept the Fact That It's Over. This doesn't mean you have to like it. Just accept the sad reality and the fact that it takes two to make a good relationship and two to let a relationship die. Let go of the other person and all the dreams you shared. This doesn't mean that you're an unworthy, bad, unlovable person. This doesn't mean that your life is ruined, even though it may hurt *a lot* right now. This accepting and letting go means realizing, often with tears, that this love was not meant to last forever.

Stay With Your Hurt Until It Heals. Cry if you need to. Write angry letters to him or her and then tear them up. Run or walk away some of your rage. Let friends and family members help you to heal. It's okay to cry and grieve for your lost relationship, but not to hate or hurt yourself. Be gentle with yourself and let your feelings happen. It's all part of the process of surviving a breakup.

Avoid Quick Fixes. When you're really hurting, there is a big temptation to grab for something, anything, that will take away the pain. Maybe this is another relationship. Beware: Love on the rebound is usually bad news. You need time to grieve, time to learn from what went wrong in the relationship so that history won't repeat itself. Or maybe you try to dull your pain with alcohol or drugs. That's not a solution. You'll just mask your pain for a little while—and create new problems for yourself. These quick fixes don't do anything to help you learn from your experience or to feel genuinely better.

Be Kind to Yourself. This is a time to be extra gentle and not criticize yourself, going over and over how you failed and what you should have done. It can help to look back and discover what you might have done different. Maybe it would have helped; maybe it wouldn't have. Some relationships can be good and loving and yet not last forever, especially when you're very young. Decide on ways you'd like to change your behavior in the future, but tell yourself, "Well, I did the best I could at the time."

Do things you enjoy with people you enjoy. Eat nutritious meals and get regular exercise (it can really help you to banish the blues!). Indulge yourself in hot baths or steamy showers or long walks in scenic places, your favorite music, an old hobby, or anything else that is good for you and that is pleasing and comforting.

Forgive the Other Person. This doesn't mean denying the fact you were hurt. This doesn't mean that the other person was right. It's just another way of letting go so that you can get on with your life. If you go around with feelings of anger and revenge, you're still tied to that other person—and you're keeping yourself unhappy. So forgive the other person. You don't have to say it out loud. Remember: this isn't for him or her. It's for *you*. You'll feel a huge weight disappear from your shoulders. And you'll have room for new happiness in your life.

Give Yourself Credit for Loving, Even If It Didn't Work Out. Being *able* to love another is important. You took the risk of being close to someone else. You gave your love and your trust. Even if that person couldn't accept this from you, you were able to give—and that is important. Look back and think of all the things you did *right* in the relationship, all the good times you had. You may find yourself crying as you think of these. But these memories are yours—and you had a large part in making these times happy. Knowing that you are a loving, giving person will give you comfort now and hope for the future.

You will survive, even though this relationship did not. You will feel better, even if that sounds impossible now. You will be stronger for having experienced both love and loss. You may never have another relationship just like the one you have lost. Especially if this was your first real love, you may never quite forget the joy and the pain the two of you shared.

But give yourself credit for sharing. And give yourself time. As you grow and discover that you make your own happiness—by living as fully and joyfully as you can whether or not there is a special love in your life at the moment—you will someday feel ready to take the risk of loving again.

CHAPTER SEVEN

Making Choices That Are Right for You

Everybody goes on and on about teenagers and drugs, sex, and drinking, and everybody seems to think choosing what to do is so easy. Adults say things like, "Just say No." They don't seem to figure out how hard it is to lose friends or get called a priss or worse. People who do drugs or drink act like they can't figure out why you wouldn't *want to do these things. It's really harder for the average teenager to decide than any of these people think. I want to do the right thing for me, but I don't always know what that is.*

Amanda K.

You're faced with so many choices in your early teen years.

In a major way, this whole book has been about making choices.

You've read about choosing to cope in positive ways with troubled feelings.

We've talked about choosing to find new ways of relating to your parents so that you can still be your own person and still be part of your family.

You've read about making choices when it comes to friendship and loyalty, about solving problems at school, about love and about laughing when there's nothing else to be done about an embarrassing situation.

But *some* choices are harder than others. Some choices can affect not only your life right now, but also your life for years to come. These choices can be life-enhancing or life-threatening. These difficult choices are about drugs, alcohol, smoking, dieting, and sex. You need to make these choices with special care. Listening to your parents' warnings about the consequences may not be enough to counteract the urgings of your peers. And listening to friends talk about the joys of sex or getting high may not be quite enough to convince you completely that these choices are right for you. "Just say No" is a good idea when in doubt, but it isn't as easy as it sounds. Saying "No" *can* mean losing friends or feeling different. People *might* make fun of you and call you a baby. You may be confronted by arguments to say "Yes" that are hard to deal with.

121

What you need to do is to find your own best reasons for saying "No" to what is harmful to you and "Yes" to life-affirming choices.

How can you start to discover the right choices for you?

When faced with a choice, ask yourself the following questions:

QUESTIONS TO ASK YOURSELF

Will This Help My Growth As a Person? This is a tricky one because some of the difficult choices seem to *make* you look grown-up. But real growth is slow and gradual. You grow by taking increasing responsibility. You grow by learning from experience what to do and say—and what *not* to do and say—in social situations.

Drinking or taking drugs to make you feel more comfortable in a crowd is a quick fix that will do nothing in the long run to make you feel more socially adept. You grow by overcoming shyness and social awkwardness little by little, with lots of small, but satisfying personal victories. Using artificial ways to ease your fears and feelings takes these little but important victories away from you. You don't grow inside. You don't learn how to face and conquer a challenge.

Quite often, we grow the most as the result of feeling pain, discomfort, and awkwardness. Finding strength within to cope with these feelings and situations is a big part of growing up.

Would Saying "Yes" to This Choice Violate Important Values of Mine? Deep down, you have feelings about what's right or wrong for you, even if you're busy rebelling against your parents and questioning their values.

This is why, for example, a lot of teens need to get drunk or feel "swept away by passion" in order to feel okay about having sex. Many teens feel that, if sex is a romantic accident, it is not immoral. On the other hand, some think that planning for sex, by getting and using reliable methods of birth control, isn't morally right *or* romantic.

Think about it: When you feel good about something, when you feel a choice is right for you, you can get a lot of pleasure from planning. When you choose to have a party or choose to go on a picnic or choose to get married, you spend time planning—with pleasure and anticipation—so that everything will be just right.

If a teen feels, deep down, that having sex is the right choice for him or her, that person will feel somewhat the same way, and will plan ahead as a way to make sure this choice will be a safe and positive one. If he or she needs to feel that sex is an accident, then this is a clue that this choice may be violating his or her own values.

In the same way, if you bow to pressure from friends to drink or try a drug or cut school or shoplift and you don't feel right about it, you'll *know*. You don't feel good inside when you're doing something that doesn't seem right to you. Even though you may be pleasing a friend, you're not pleasing yourself. You may be hurting your own self-image. You may be exposing yourself to unnecessary pain and problems just because someone else thinks you ought to do something.

There are ways you can please your friends without hurting yourself. Putting your own feelings and values first isn't selfish. It's necessary! You need to make choices *you* can live with!

Is This Choice Kind to Me . . . and to Others? Some choices may feel good for the moment, but may not be good for you in the long run. If a choice doesn't enhance your self-esteem, if it exposes you to more problems and dangers, it isn't kind to you. If it also means that you'll be hurting others, like parents and friends who care about you and trust you, it also isn't kind.

For example, drinking and drugs can dull your emotional pain temporarily, but can end up making you more depressed and facing more problems, including risks to your health, well-being, self-esteem, and even to your life.

Dieting so severely that you acquire the shape of a nine-year-old boy may satisfy an immediate urge to look trendy and fit into a certain jean size. But this dieting can stunt your growth, interfere with your hormone production, and may expose you to special health dangers if you develop an eating disorder like anorexia nervosa or bulimia.

Agreeing to cut school with a friend can be fun and deliciously forbidden for the moment, but may cause both of you problems in the future. The same can be said for shoplifting. The temporary joys can't begin to measure up to the pain and embarrassment of getting caught and facing uncomfortable consequences.

What Are the Consequences of This Choice? Sometimes the consequences of these tough choices seem uncertain or very far off.

Maybe you've heard about people getting lung cancer as the result of smoking, but that's years away and, besides, it doesn't happen to everybody.

Maybe you've read the statistics on teen pregnancy, but you know some kids who have sex without birth control and they've been lucky. You have every reason to believe you'll be lucky, too.

Maybe you've read about people who can't stop dieting and manage to starve themselves practically to death. But you're not planning to starve yourself. You just want to lose ten or twenty pounds, that's all, so you can get into size 4 jeans.

Maybe you've seen shows on TV about teenage alcoholics and alcohol-related accidents, but, for heavens sake, a few drinks at a party once a week won't cause any problems—or will they?

Too often, teens hope for the best, assume they'll be lucky, or just try not to think about the most serious possible consequences of a choice. "It can't happen to me!" is quite often followed by "I didn't think it would happen to me!"

To make choices that are right for you, you need to realize and think about the most serious possible consequences of a given choice. Maybe these won't happen to you. But maybe they will. Realistically, would you choose to have to deal with a serious problem like an alcohol or drug addiction or a pregnancy? Is this choice really worth the risks—to you?

Do I Have Enough Information to Make a Responsible Choice? How do you know if a choice is right for you? How do you know if it is worth the risks—or how to reduce the risks?

You need information. You need to know exactly what you're choosing and why. You need to know how this choice could affect you right now, and how it could affect your life in the future. You need to know how to reduce the risks when possible. And you need to think about *other* choices that could give you good feelings without the bad consequences.

These tough, important choices are, all too often, made without enough information. That's not fair to you.

You owe it to yourself to know what you're choosing. You owe it to yourself to think, not only of the benefits, but also of the consequences. Then, based on this information, you can decide what's right for you.

If you fall into a certain action or activity by just letting it happen or because you didn't fully realize what you were getting into or it was all an accident (really!), you're *still* making a choice. But it may not be the best one for you.

These choices are far too important to be left to chance. You owe it to yourself to choose freely—and wisely.

THE TOUGH CHOICES

Drugs

The Benefits: You may feel more at ease in awkward or scary situations. You may feel accepted by a group at last. You may feel less pain, at least for the moment.

The Consequences: You might get labeled and stuck into your school's "druggie" group, and it might be very hard to shake this label if you change your mind about using drugs.

Using and abusing drugs can also complicate your life. Chances are, you will not function as well at home or at school. You won't grow emotionally since you're using drugs to avoid painful feelings instead of facing these feelings and learning to deal with them.

More to the point, drugs are a danger to your health.

Crack, a form of cocaine, for example, is really bad news. The high from this drug is very short before you crash into a depression. Then you're stuck with needing to take more and more crack at shorter intervals to keep this depression from overwhelming you. Crack and cocaine can also kill—even the first time you try it, if you happen to be especially unlucky. This happens because the drug causes the blood vessels to narrow, reducing the blood flow to the heart, and there can be a disturbance of the heart's natural rhythm. In this way, a healthy teenager could have a heart attack or heart failure due to heart rhythm irregularities. Cocaine can also affect the brain in a way that causes potentially fatal seizures. And those *most* at risk are healthy young people.

Even a drug like marijuana is dangerous. A lot of people consider this a pretty harmless drug. But they shouldn't. Today's marijuana is much more potent than the grass young people smoked in the sixties. And new medical findings have revealed some alarming facts.

For example, habitual pot smoking can be even more damaging to the lungs than cigarette smoking. This can mean cancer later on, but bouts of bronchitis and lots of chest colds right now.

Heavy use of marijuana can also disrupt hormone production in both males and females, cause problems with concentration, sleep disorders, and personality changes.

And these are only two of the drugs that are common among young drug users.

You've probably heard more than you've ever wanted to hear about the dangers of drugs from school programs and from your parents. So there's just one more thought you might want to consider when making a choice about whether or not to use a drug: Growing up is challenging enough. Why make it any harder?

Alcohol

The Benefits: Alcohol may make you feel less shy and uptight when you're with others. You may feel that drinking makes you look more mature, and that you're more accepted by others when you can join in and drink just like one of the crowd.

The Consequences: Talk about total embarrassment! What would you think if you got drunk and made a fool of yourself or, even worse, got sick and threw up in front of someone you were trying to impress?? And that's just a *minor* consequence!

Alcohol, like drugs, can also interfere with your growth as a person, with your life at school and at home. If you drink to escape your shyness or your pain, think twice. Those feelings are only masked, not resolved, by alcohol use. Some problems are better toughed out than blocked out by booze.

The health risks also cannot be underestimated. These can happen and you don't have to wait a long time for your health to suffer. Teens are more vulnerable to problem drinking than any other age group. Why? Because your body weight is lower than an adult's (so alcohol enters your bloodstream in a shorter time and in a less diluted form), because your alcohol tolerance is lower, and because teens tend to drink more alcohol more often and may also combine drinking with drug use.

Researchers have found that teenagers can develop from problem drinkers to alcoholics much more quickly than adults. And the health problems that go along with alcoholism—like malnutrition (from drinking instead of eating) and damage to the brain, liver, pancreas, and central nervous system—can occur more quickly. One alcoholism counselor cites a recent study showing that someone who starts drinking heavily at age 13 (three or more drinks, three or more times a week) can develop life-threatening cirrhosis of the liver by age 23.

And drinking and driving can be the most rapidly fatal combination of all. It is estimated that alcohol-related accidents (auto crashes, drownings, and other accidental deaths) are responsible for nearly 75 percent of teen deaths.

Most young people experiment with drinking at one time or another. And many people can handle a drink now and then. But those people tend to be more mature and sure of themselves to begin with. The people who most *need* alcohol to feel good and comfortable and forget their cares are the ones most at risk for problem drinking.

Alcohol can cause many more problems than it solves. Teen alcoholism is no myth and no joke. It can embarrass you. It can destroy your health and your relationships. It can kill.

Smoking

The Benefits: You feel cool and sophisticated. You have something to do with your hands when you're in a social gathering. You feel that smoking helps to control your weight by putting a finishing touch to a meal and by reducing in-between meal snacking.

The Consequences: Smoking can shorten your life considerably—by six to nine years on the average. Smokers are not only more likely to get lung cancer, but also to get cancers of the lips, mouth, bladder, esophagus, and uterus. Smokers are also at much greater risk of having heart attacks and strokes, as well as the disabling respiratory disease emphysema.

That all may be some years away and may not mean much to you now. But wait!

There are some consequences that *can* affect your life now and in the near future.

Smoking gives you bad breath, stains your teeth, makes your clothes and hair smell awful. Your skin will age rapidly—so that you may get wrinkles some 20 years before many of your nonsmoking peers. And, if you're female, you need to know that women who smoke are almost twice as likely to miscarry their babies, have a stillborn baby, or a live baby who is smaller than normal.

As a smoker, you will join a beleaguered minority. According to the American Cancer Society, most teens guess that the majority of people their age smoke. Actually, only 30 percent of teenage boys and 27 percent of teenage girls smoke. In case you hadn't noticed, smoking is not really IN among the general public. More and more restaurants are banning smokers. Some airline flights prohibit smoking as well. And a lot of people find the practice objectionable, especially since new studies show that side-stream smoke—the smoke that other people inhale as a result of your smoking—can be hazardous to their health.

Why start a habit that's going to harm you and others—and expose you to hostility and hassles everywhere you go?

Dieting

The Benefits: You'll be thin and, you feel, more popular. You'll better fit the ideal for weight-conscious activities like ballet or gymnastics or wrestling. Trendy clothes will look good on you. You'll avoid getting fat (which, at your school, may lead to social oblivion).

The Consequences: Some people may think that putting dieting in the same league with drugs and drinking and smoking is silly. But it's a real risk for young teenagers.

This is a time—at the height of puberty—when girls put on an average of 20 pounds to gain a more adult female shape. Upset and afraid that boys won't like them, they start dieting severely as young as the age of nine.

What can severe dieting do to you?

It can stunt your growth and interfere with physical development. In a study of young people nine to seventeen who had been seriously dieting, doctors found that these teens were not only underweight, but also underdeveloped and shorter than their nondieting classmates. In the case of those already in their teens, this shortness was permanent because their bone growth had been stunted at a crucial time. (For someone trying to be super-skinny in hopes of being a model, this could be really bad news. Models are generally much taller than average—at least 5'7". Stunting your growth could be a much bigger obstacle to your dream than being a little heavy.)

Severe dieting can interfere with female hormone production and menstrual periods. (You need a certain level of fat in your body to produce the hormones that make regular menstrual periods possible.) Before you start considering this a blessing, you need to know that some doctors fear that years of insufficient hormone production may lead to premature bone loss and weakness.

Severe dieting can also make you vulnerable to serious eating disorders like anorexia nervosa (compulsive dieting and exercising to the point of starvation or near starvation), and bulimia (binging on food and then getting rid of it by vomiting and, possibly, using a lot of laxatives as well). Both of these disorders can be life-threatening.

Constant dieting can also lead to compulsive overeating—and serious over-weight problems. You feel so deprived by severe dieting that you lose control and eat everything in sight, gain back all the weight you lost, and then go on another diet. This unhealthy cycle, called "yo-yo dieting," is very stressful and unhealthy.

Even if you don't develop serious health problems as the result of dieting, it can interfere with a lot of good experiences. If you think you're not worth knowing unless you're a certain small size, and if you hate yourself everytime you put on a pound or two, this low opinion of yourself can lead to a lot of unhappiness. If you're always on a diet and can never join your friends for burgers or pizza or a picnic on the beach, you're missing out on a lot of fun. (You don't have to eat a lot when you're with your friends. You may even want to bring healthy food of your own. But when you get obsessed with dieting and weight loss, you tend to *avoid* any circumstances that involve food—and you can miss out on a lot of fun that way.)

A better choice: Check with your doctor to see if you really are overweight and get his or her recommendations for an eating plan that will give you the nutrients you need for growth while still maintaining a healthy weight. Whether you're overweight or not, eating sensible, well-balanced meals and getting a reasonable amount of exercise can help you to keep your weight where you want it—without the social isolation, deprivation, disappointment, and danger of severe dieting.

Sex

The Benefits: You may feel, at least for a time, very close to another, getting the hugs, warmth, and attention you've always wanted. You may feel loved and needed. You may feel grown up and sophisticated.

The Consequences: Sex does not guarantee love. It does not make you more grown-up or wiser. It does not create an unbreakable emotional bond between two people, especially if loving commitment did not exist before sex took place.

And sex *does* have some serious consequences.

If you have sex without using birth control, pregnancy is a real risk. You can get pregnant the first time you ever have sex. You can get pregnant even if he promises to pull out in time. And having a baby when you're a preteen or in your early teens is not only a health risk for you and the baby, it is also a life-changing risk for you.

Your life will change drastically. Now you will lose a lot of the freedom you've tried so hard to win because you'll be tied down with a baby. (Babies can be a joy, but they *do* require constant care, some of it very tiring for a new parent.) Statistically, a teenage girl who has a baby and keeps it is much more likely to drop out of school and spend a lifetime in poverty. (Is that what you really want for yourself—and your future children?)

Having sex, especially if you don't follow safe-sex guidelines by using condoms and avoiding high-risk people and practices, can expose you to many different sexually transmitted diseases. These diseases can not only be embarrassing, uncomfortable, and inconvenient, but some of them can also threaten your future fertility, your health, *and* your life! AIDS happens to all kinds of people. It is, in fact, the seventh leading cause of death for young people between the ages of 15 and 24. (Since the incubation period for AIDS may be several years, a 15-year-old victim may have acquired the disease as a preteen or in the early teens.) Contrary to what you may have heard, AIDS (and other serious sexually transmitted diseases) don't just happen to gay people or to people who run around with a lot of different partners. These diseases can also happen to those who have had sex with only one person (if that one person happens to be infected). You can't afford *not* to be careful. Your health and even your life could depend upon your cautious choices.

And yet another risk remains: the risk to your feelings. Having sex before you're emotionally ready . . . or with the wrong person . . . or with someone who was just using you (when you thought it was true love) . . . or when you feel forced . . . or to keep a relationship going (but you end up losing that person anyway), can all be hazardous to your good feelings about yourself. Girls are especially vulnerable to emotional fallout from early sexual experiences.

A recent study of junior high students at a large midwestern school found that sexual activity for girls was linked with lower self-esteem. These girls may have engaged in sex at an early age in an effort to feel better about themselves, but their experiences, instead, make them feel even worse.

Sex *cannot* cure a self-esteem problem. You can't feel good about yourself if you're violating an important value of yours or if you're allowing yourself to be used or if you're desperately seeking sexual experiences just to be held and feel loved, if only temporarily.

Like the other attempts to mask pain, sex too soon can interfere with your ability to grow, to feel good about yourself, and to relate in vital, nonsexual ways with the opposite sex (and that is a very important part of building good, lasting love relationships). You need to understand each other's feelings and develop a strong sense of caring and loyalty. You need to learn to talk with each other and work out your differences. And sex is no shortcut to this process. In fact, having sex instead of relating in other ways can make you less likely and able to have a lasting love relationship.

In the right circumstances, sex can be a real joy, an affirmation of love, but it is not the *only* way to show your love. It is no proof of love. Having the courage to work through your differences and to be there for each other through a crisis is a much better proof of love. Being loyal to each other, enjoying a concert together, taking a long walk together, laughing together, working for a cause together—all of these are ways of sharing love that do much more for your own growth and that of your relationship than just rushing into sex.

Making Your Own Best Choices

After reading all the advice and statistics and hearing what your parents and your friends think, only *you* can make the tough choices in your own life. Only *you* can decide whether or not to have that drink or smoke that cigarette or have sex for the first time. But, when you're thinking over your choice, it makes sense to choose whatever is best for you in all ways: emotionally, physically, spiritually, and socially.

These important choices aren't easy. Sometimes your feelings and insecurities will urge you in a certain direction. Sometimes your body will (silently) cry "Yes!" while your mind cautions "No!" And there will always be classmates and acquaintances and even close friends who try to convince you that making a certain choice is the cool or sophisticated or grown-up thing to do, despite your own misgivings.

You can make your choices a little easier by avoiding problem situations as much as possible and looking at peer pressure as a learning experience.

For example, avoid running with a fast crowd whose choices and feelings are quite different from yours. If you like one or two people in this group, see them individually. (It's easier to say "No" to one or two people than to a whole crowd.) Avoid unsupervised parties where you *know* drugs, alcohol, or sexual adventures will abound. Don't go out with or get into a car with someone who is drunk or stoned—or has a reputation for that sort of behavior.

If people laugh at you or call you a baby, don't believe them. Having the courage to be different or to have your own opinion is a sign of maturity. And, besides, you won't be *that* different. Most people your age don't use or abuse substances or have sex. It just *seems* like everyone else is doing these things. A lot of people brag about all kinds of things they haven't really done just to avoid being teased.

Coping with peer pressure and making the choices that are best for you can help you to begin thinking for yourself—and that's a great start toward a healthy, mature future.

How can you say "No" without making a scene or making everyone hate you?

It's best to keep it friendly and low-key. Don't rant and rave about the evils of drugs and drink. Experiment with less noticeable turn-downs like:

"I'd rather not . . ."

"I'm allergic to that . . ."

"I tried it and didn't care for it . . ."

"I'm not ready to have sex yet, even though I care very much about you."

"I don't feel comfortable with strict diets. I'm trying to get healthy and fit with exercise."

"I get sick when I drink . . ."

"My parents would kill me. Seriously, they'd ground me for the rest of the year."

"No, thanks, not now . . ."

"I feel better when I don't (drink, do drugs, smoke) and I want to make the most of this time with you."

Saying "No" to quick fixes and other choices that seem to alleviate pain, if only temporarily, is especially hard if you're feeling bad about yourself and your life right now.

Even if you have a lot of reasons to want to escape your painful feelings, even if you feel unloved, unnoticed, unattractive, and immature, there are some very positive choices you can make.

- You can make healthy good looks a goal by eating nutritious, well-balanced meals and working out regularly. There is a special attractiveness about a person who cares enough to keep in good shape and practice careful grooming. When you take care of yourself physically, you'll feel better inside and out!

- You can make the choice to be a good friend, to be a kind, supportive, fun, caring companion. In doing this, you don't have to go against any of your own values. You don't have to be a drinking companion. You don't have to get stoned with another. You don't have to have sex if you're not ready. You can show your love in many wonderful ways by just being yourself. This will be enough for the people who truly care about you.

- You can choose to look for love and caring in positive ways: from people who care about your growth. Real friends don't *want* you to do anything that's harmful or illegal or that makes you feel bad about yourself. They want you to do well, to be healthy. Even if your choices are quite different from theirs, they can tolerate these differences and even appreciate your strength in being your own person.

Do you have the feeling that no one really cares? You'd be surprised if you could see into the hearts of those around you. If you don't have any close friends at school, there are a number of *potential* friends who would bring a lot of joy into your life if you could reach out to them and give them a chance.

If you and your parents can't express love (or don't feel much love for each other at the moment), there are other adults who care: other relatives, a favorite teacher, a coach, a choir director, a youth counselor at your church or synagogue, a neighbor, a special family friend.

If you have yet to find the love of your life (or even if you *have* but he or she doesn't know it yet), you can enjoy the love of friends of both sexes. And you never know: out of one of these friendships something very special could grow. Lasting love often comes from friendship—and friendships, in themselves, can be special and lifelong.

- You can choose to do what's best for *you*. You deserve the best. And when you really think about it, you *know* what's best for you. What you need to do is to listen to your feelings. Listen to those who really care about you. Get as much information as you can. Then make your choice. Make it wisely and with love for the special person you are right now—and the wonderfully strong and unique person you're growing to be.

CHAPTER EIGHT

Your Dreams for the Future: They're Important!

I'm 13 and love to sing. I dream about being a singing star someday. But my family makes fun of me and tells me I'd better get real and learn how to type. It hurts my feelings!

Angie A.

I'm on the basketball team and it's the best thing that ever happened to me. I have this ambition to play professionally. But my dad laughs and says, "Forget it. There are no white basketball players except on the Boston Celtics. And what makes you think they'd want you?" But I hope they do because I sure want to. Is this a silly dream like everyone says?

Ben D.

Is it wrong to dream about getting married and having kids and not having a really big career? My friends say it's stupid because everyone works and most people get divorced. The thing is, relationships are more important to me than making lots of money or being famous. Am I wrong to dream about this?

Debra T.

My friends all want to be doctors or lawyers or have their own businesses and make lots of money. I want to be a teacher. Everyone makes fun of me and says that's wimpy and I won't make very much money. My parents say I'll probably change my mind a hundred times before I'm ready to start working because I'm only 13 now. But I really think this is what I want. Can you be my age and know what you want and be right about it even when other people think you're wrong?

John N.

Your dreams matter—even if other people don't believe in them.

People discount your dreams for a lot of reasons.

Parents get protective, especially if you aspire to a career that is very chancy and competitive like sports or entertainment. They know that many people who are truly gifted never make it to the top or even into professional ranks at all. And they want to protect you from disappointment, disillusionment, and the pain of setting your sights on a goal that may not be attainable, even if you're very good and work hard for years.

This just means they love you. It doesn't mean you should stop dreaming.

Sometimes your friends may diminish your dreams because they don't match their own dreams—and they need security in numbers. Someone with different dreams may cause them to question their own—and that's scary. So if you dream of being a wife and mother and your friends tell you that isn't a realistic dream, maybe it *isn't* what they want, but it could be just right for you.

Just because your dreams are different from those of your friends is no reason to stop dreaming.

It's true that you can't build a life entirely on dreams. You *do* need some practical skills and a good education, whatever your plans for the future. Maybe you *will* become a sports star. The better you are at math, the better you will be able to handle your money. The better you are in speech and English, the more articulate you will be in interviews.

And learning to type doesn't mean getting stuck in a secretarial job if that's not what you want. Typing well can help you excel at computer work. It can also pay the rent while you try to make it as a singer or actress. Knowing how to type will help you to do better in high school and college. It's just another life skill that can be very handy—even if you don't have big plans for a career. Everyone needs basic work skills to give them more choices in their lives and, in some instances, to make more exciting dreams a reality.

If you dream of being a homemaker and mother, studying hard now can help you get a good grasp of school subjects so you can help your kids do well in school. It also helps to have work skills, even if you don't plan on a career, because you never know what will happen. Maybe you won't find the right person to marry until long after graduation. Maybe illness or a job layoff could mean that you will need to help support the family for a while. And if you want your kids to go to college, you may need to work some of the time to put money aside for them.

You never know exactly what directions your life will take.

Some people seem to grow up knowing exactly what they want to do with their lives—and everything turns out just right.

Other people don't discover their real strengths and talents until they're older, maybe even after having a job that didn't work out.

And many people have things happen to them that they never expected: they don't meet someone to marry or they get divorced or a spouse dies or they don't have the family they always dreamed of having. Of course, not all unexpected turns of fate are sad. Sometimes people surprise themselves with their own success. They discover talents they never knew they had or find joy in careers they couldn't have imagined when they were younger.

So it makes sense to pay attention to reality and learn everything you can to give yourself the best possible choices for the future.

This can mean doing the best you can in school right now, not necessarily avoiding classes like math. (People who avoid math or science courses in junior high and high school can limit their possibilities in college and/or many career choices. Don't decide too soon that math and science are not for you at all.)

This can also mean learning basic skills like typing or using a computer, even if this doesn't seem very exciting, just because these are good skills to know.

This can mean leaving your mind open to all kinds of future dreams and possibilities.

Facing reality does NOT mean losing your present dreams. They're important in special ways. What makes your dreams so important?

Your Dreams Bring Excitement to Your Life. They can give you a high that no drink or drug possibly can. It's not only exciting to dream of the future, but also to prepare for it right now. So if you love basketball or music or acting or dance or writing or computer programming, you may already be doing what you dream of pursuing as a career in the future. And the joy you get from learning these skills and pursuing them as special hobbies and interests is immediate—and can last a lifetime, whether or not you ever become a professional.

For example, many people love to ice skate and many young people have Olympic dreams. There are very, very few young skaters who go on to become Brian Boitano or Katerina Witt or Debi Thomas. But many find that they have a skill that brings them joy (and great exercise) for life!

I have a dear friend, Orlie—my family's next-door neighbor when I was growing up—who, after he retired from his teaching career, got more seriously into his ice skating hobby, something that he had enjoyed since his Canadian childhood. Orlie is now over 70 and a competitive ice dancer in his age division. He trains daily with joy and vigor and travels all over the U.S. for competitions. It just goes to show that life is always exciting when you're doing what you love—and it's never too late to pursue and fulfill a dream!

Your Dreams Can Help You to Discover Your Own Uniqueness. Your dreams can tell you a lot about your personal priorities. If you want to be a teacher, you may be the kind of person who puts the satisfaction of helping others ahead of making lots of money. If you dream of making lots of money, discovering why may reveal some important things about you. Maybe you feel that having money will give you more choices in your life—maybe choosing to take time to travel or to stay home with young children or share your wealth with those less fortunate. Maybe you're feeling very deprived right now and think that money will make everything all right. (If that is the case, it may be time to think about why some very rich people are unhappy with their lives and think about some *other* dreams that might also bring you joy. This doesn't mean letting go of your dreams of being rich, but being open to all kinds of goals for the future.)

Having dreams—and paying attention to these dreams—can help you to discover what's really important to you—and what isn't.

Your Dreams Can Give You Hope. Hope can see you through a lot of hard times. Hope can keep you plugging away when school is incredibly boring. Hope can help you to rise above family problems and troubled feelings. Hope can help you to make wise choices right now. If you have a dream for your future, it's easier to make sacrifices, to say "No" to choices that aren't right for you, because you know that there will be much more to your life than just today—and that choices you make today can influence whether your dreams survive tomorrow. Hope can give you the strength to do things you never thought you could do. Hope can help you to take risks worth taking and grow in ways that make you a better, stronger, more compassionate and fascinating person. Hope can help you look past the pain and uncertainty of today to your dreams for tomorrow.

In time, some of your dreams may change. As we grow and change, some of our dreams change, too. You may find yourself letting go of some, not with sadness, but because you have found wonderful new dreams.

Making choices and changes as you grow up doesn't mean ceasing to dream or losing your dreams. It can mean *finding* many of your dreams coming true—and discovering exciting new dreams for your ever-growing future!

INDEX

Index

Carrie!

I got this book
hoping it would show
you that being a teenager
isn't easy, but it's greatest
time of your life, so enjoy!!

I'm always here to talk
about anything.

Love your Buddy,

Isa